STRATEGY FOR INTEGRATED AREA DEVELOPMENT

By the same author

Man and Land in South Asia (Concept)

Impact of a Metropolitan City in the Surrounding Region (Concept)

STRATEGY FOR INTEGRATED AREA DEVELOPMENT

Case Study of North Kanara District
(Karnataka)

(Report of a Research Project sponsored by the Indian Council of Social Science Research, New Delhi)

L. S. BHAT

I.C.S.S.R. Consultant
C.D. Deshpande

CONCEPT PUBLISHING COMPANY, NEW DELHI-110015

The Indian Council of Social Science Research gave the financial support towards the publication of this work. However, the responsibility for the contents of the book-facts, opinions, conclusions, etc, - is entirely that of the author and not of the ICSSR.

ISBN 81-7022-198-6

First Published 1988

L.S. Bhat (b.1931

Published by

Naurang Rai
Concept Publishing Company
H-13, Bali Nagar
NEW DELHI-110015 (India)

Printed at

Taj Press
A 35/4 Maya Puri
NEW DELHI

TO MY TEACHER

PROFESSOR C.D. DESHPANDE

PREFACE

Integrated Rural Development Strategy formulated in the Five Year Plans of economic development in India have the essential aim of increasing agricultural productivity, creating employment opportunities and providing essential facilities and amenities for the people - particularly the rural poor. The concept is akin to that of the Area Development strategy at the Block and District levels. Spatial approach is implied in this concept with emphasis on physical planning of agricultural landuse and human settlements as both these components are *area* or *location* specific. Preparation of a resource inventory, and identification of growth centres are considered essential in the preparation of area development plans. There is thus considerable confusion between the spatial development framework on the one hand and certain ingredients of the development framework as mentioned above.

The present exercise is by no means exhaustive. Yet, the sharp contrasts within the District and the centrifugal pattern of spatial organisation of the economy bring out the inadequacies in the manner in which Integrated Rural Development or Area Development Plans at the Block and District levels are formulated and implemented. The study area with its diversified resource base calls for an intensive survey using village level data for each Development Block/Taluka in the context of the innovative experiment in decentralised planning that has just been initiated by the Government of Karnataka.

For statistical data and other information my thanks are due to the official agencies at the District and State level: The District Statistical Office, Revenue Department, Department of Industry,

District and Regional Planning Unit of the Planning Department, Government of Karnataka.

I thank the Indian Council of Social Science Research for providing financial support for conducting this study. The Indian Statistical Institute, Delhi Centre provided all the facilities from time to time.

My thanks are due to Shri P. Subrahmanyam and Shri P.V. Rao who have assisted me in the initial stages of the work particularly in processing the secondary data.

I thank Shri. A.N. Sharma, Lecturer at the Institute for his generous assistance and co-operation at every stage of the work including finalisation of maps.

I thank Shri Mehar Lal and Shri V.P. Sharma for their excellent typing of the report.

NEW DELHI L.S. BHAT
January 26, 1988

CONTENTS

PREFACE 7

LIST OF ILLUSTRATIONS 10

LIST OF TABLES 11

ONE: INTRODUCTION 13

TWO: THE STUDY AREA 20

THREE:PHYSICAL SETTING 29

FOUR: RESOURCE BASE 34

FIVE: SPATIAL ORGANISATION OF ECONOMIC ACTIVITIES INFRASTRUCTURAL FACILITIES AND AMENITIES AND INDUSTRIES 64

SIX: SUMMARY AND CONCLUSIONS 92

REFERENCES 98

INDEX 103

LIST OF ILLUSTRATIONS

1. Spatial and Locational Dimensions in Regional Development 15
2. North Kanara District in its Regional Setting 22
3. North Kanara District : political administrative setting before 1953 23
4. North Kanara District : Places of Historical importance 26
5. North Kanara District : Sub-regions 30
6. North Kanara District : Net area sown (1983-84) 36
7. North Kanara District : Cropping Pattern (1983-84) 38
8. North Kanara District : Forest (1983-84) 42
9. North Kanara District : Population Growth Rate (1971-81) 44
10. North Kanara District : Population Density 46
11. North Kanara District : Literacy 1981 51
12. North Kanara District : Proportion of rural settlements and population - settlements of less than 500 persons (1981) 56
13. North Kanara District : Urbanisation 1981 61
14. North Kanara District : Pattern of growth of Towns 1971-81 62
15. North Kanara District : Transport routes 65
16. North Kanara District : Industrial Structure 72
17. North Kanara District : Locational Pattern of Small-Scale Industries 73
18. Karnataka : Perspectives in spatial organisation of sub-regional economies 94

LIST OF TABLES

1. North Kanara District : Sub-regions 32
2. North Kanara District : Spatial variations in Land use (1983-84) 35
3. North Kanara District : Cropping Pattern (1983-84) 39
4. North Kanara District : Pattern of Growth of Population (1971-81) 45
5. North Kanara District : Population Density and Growth rate (1971-81) 47
6. North Kanara District : Sex ratio (1981) 49
7. North Kanara District : Pattern of Literacy 52
8. North Kanara District : Rural Population Distribution in different size range of settlements (1981) - sub-regional variations 54
9. North Kanara District : Distribution of Population in different size range of settlements (taluka-wise) 1981 55
10. North Kanara District : Pattern of urbanization (taluka-wise 1971) 58
11. North Kanara District : Pattern of urbanization (Taluka-wise 1981) 59
12. North Kanara District : Population size and pattern of growth of towns (1901-1981) 60
13. North Kanara District : Roads (1977-78) 66
14. North Kanara District : Extent of Electrification (1977-78) 68
15. North Kanara District : Educational Facilities (1977-78) 69
16. North Kanara District : Banking facilities (1977-78) 70
17. North Kanara District : Postal facilities (1977-78) 70

18. North Kanara District : Health facilities (1977-78) 71
19. North Kanara District : Regional characteristics in composition of small scale industry 74
20. North Kanara District : Pattern of concentration of small scale industries 75
21. North Kanara District : Small scale industries 76
22. North Kanara District : Types of small scale industries 80
23. North Kanara District : Weightages to social facilities and economic activities 82
24. North Kanara District : Population size and rank of settlements based on composite score 83

ONE

Introduction

Integrated Area Planning has been emphasized in the Five Year Plans of Economic Development in India since the beginning of the Fourth Five Year Plan.[1] It had its roots in the objectives and strategies formulated in the First Year Plan itself which stated that the District continues to be basic unit of planning and pivot of administration.[2] Re-organisation of Districts to render them more viable for administration and planning then became the focus of attention; and several studies were made in the re-adjustment of District boundaries.[3] Re-organisation of Districts has been made by State Governments and new Districts have been carved out e.g. in Kerala, Maharashtra, Bihar, Haryana to mention a few. Some of these were more on political considerations than according to the felt need of the people or the planning and administrative requirements. Regional or area approach to planning was also noted in the Second and Third Five Year Plans which stated that for certain sectors of the economy such as agriculture, the agro-climatic regions would be more realistic than adoption of the the Linguistic State with sharp intra-State differences and inter-State (in contiguous areas stretching across the State boundary) differences in physical and agronomic conditions as 'regions'. Likewise, the strategy for minimisation of regional imbalances in development spelt out at length, in general terms, and the statement about the complementarity of the sectoral and regional perspectives of development (1961-76) in the Third Five Year Plan brought to focus the wide gulf that exists as between *sectoral* and *temporal* dimensions of the Development Plan operated through the different tiers of the political-administrative hierarchy (treated as regional framework) from top downward and spatial planning using the concept of region and regional development planning.[4] The latter implies that the development process is initiated *in* or *on* the geographic surface which comprises the *areal* and *locational* components, e.g. agricultural land or physical resources in general and the human settlements (Fig.1).[5] Geographers are familiar with the concept that regional or area approach serves to co-ordinate the development planning activities carried out by individual departments; and that it could be the basis for planning at different regional or areas levels - according to the importance of economic activities whether they are of national, regional or local importance. This aspect of formulation of objectives and strategies for development of activities appropriate to different scales of areas and economic activities is a missing link in the attempts made by geographers in conducting studies relating to planning at the District and Block levels. Before attempting a study related to planning at these levels of areas it is necessary to ask ourselves as to whether a regional or area study should precede the study oriented to planning. Regional geography to regional survey for planning is a logical step and this applies to area planning also.

Development process - a spatial view :

The national economy is organised in the geographic space, and yet, the complexity of spatial organisation of the economy as it is rooted to the historical and political aspects on the one hand and the resource base and patterns of development on the other has not received adequate attention. The *regional* or *spatial dimension* itself has been elusive and interpreted by different but related fields of physical and social sciences. Economics by virtue of its early stage of development has not given the lead to the introduction of "location and space economy" in the context of economic development. The process of development operating in the geographic surface is not seen in its dynamic aspects of "functional organisation of the formal space" and essential principle of spatial organisation of the economy at the *macro*, *meso* or *micro* levels. This idea of space and spatial organisation of the economy has of late been further clarified by elaborating it under ' location and space economy' (Lsch and Isard) and 'location and human interaction' (Haggett).[6] In early writings of sociologists (La Play) the concept of place <—> work <—> folk or environment <—> economic activity <—> people finds its expressions which have been demonstrated in the form of 'a spatial development model' (*norm* of development in accordance with the intrinsic conditions of the given area e.g. Valley Section of Patrick Geddes).[7] The question arises as to whether social scientists engaged in regional or area studies for planning should not attempt to construct a similar spatial development model at the micro level and concretise the same by working out quantitative norms appropriate to each activity e.g. livestock carrying capacity of land suitable for grass and grazing as against the existing subsistence cereal farming in certain foot hill areas.

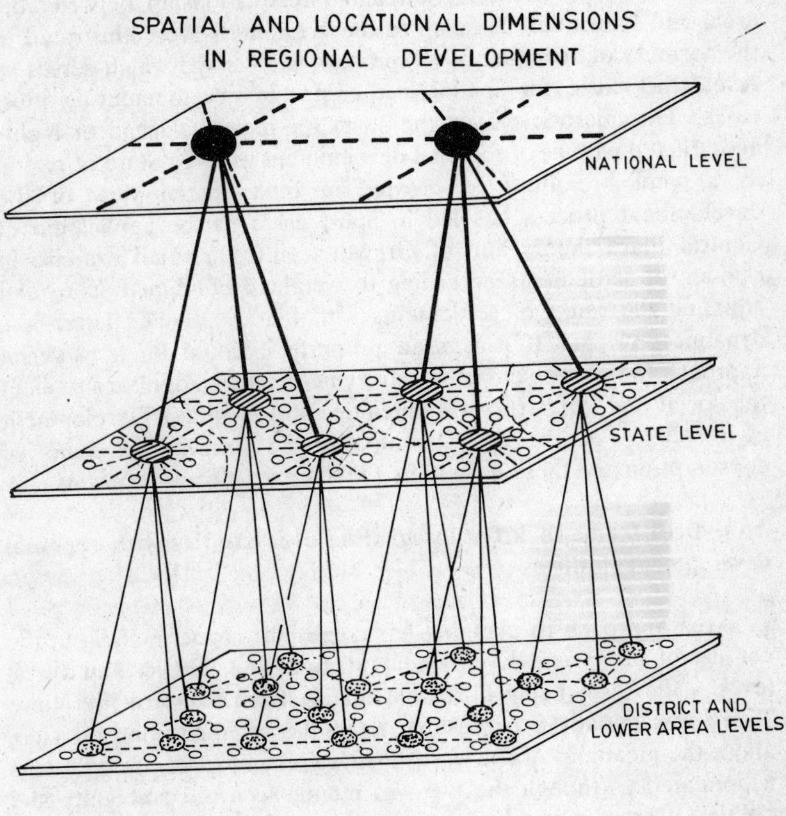

Fig. 1

Similarly, the development process gets initiated by the formation of 'nodes' which are the basis for spatial integration e.g. rural-urban integration, agriculture and processing activities based on it etc. This spatial view has another connotation at the micro level in that the concept of physical planning of land uses takes note of land qualities and their interrelationship in the physical or topographical characteristics e.g. land units and land system based on geomorphological processes. In rugged terrain, a small river basin could be the best illustration of vertical zonation of land uses starting from the valley floor to the water-shed.

This concept of interaction and interrelationship between the areal and locational elements of the economy is best illustrated in the formula of structure <–> process <–> stage which serves to reveal the cause for spatial inequalities in development in most cases. The micro-level sets the stage for more balanced or highly accentuated pattern of regional development within a State or nation as a whole. Failure to provide in built spatial view of the development process has led in many cases to the application of Central Place theory and of Growth Centres a ritual exercise in ranking of settlements according to weighted combined score and equating the ranks of settlements with hierarchy.[8] The latter is a dynamic concept. If it is used properly it could be a powerful approach to the problem of selectivity in the choice of places to meet the social and infrastructural amenities and facilities. Development of resources of the area create demand for various items of consumption and these have to be provided in selected locations.

Analytical framework for integrating area studies with regional development studies:

Area approach to planning has come into vogue in India in the context of preparing development plans at the District and Block levels - the term being borrowed mainly from Western literature. There was initially a confusion, as in the regional concept itself, about the meanings of the words *area,region* and *space*. At one stage it appeared as though the use was mainly to avoid ambiguity and political overtones attached to the problem of regional development.

Though *area approach* was implied in planning at Block and District levels the approach to the preparation of the Block and Districts plans does not reflect area approach in its content. Often, it is the same process of 'putting together' the financial outlays and sectoral targets (sectors not necessarily being the same as sectoral dimensions of the State and the National plan). At the micro level, the economic activities in their areal and locational setting serve to evaluate the backward and forward linkages of activities.

Development Block, the District and sub-regions within States comprising groups of Districts/Development Blocks provide a basis for planning close to ground reality integrating and co-ordinating the plans, at these area levels.[9] It is against this background too that the merits of decentralised planning using sub-regions within States can be appreciated. Devolution of administrative powers from the state level to sub-regional levels is necessary for effective implementation of this strategy.[10]

Approach to integrated area planning

That all planning is for planning of land use and settlements can be best illustrated in the approach to integrated area planning. The areas comprising its physical resources and human settlements and their attributes need systematic analysis in terms of their spatial distribution, pattern of association and potentials. The concept of a resource inventory needs elaboration in a spatial context unlike a huge data inventory that is now being built up at different area levels and Departments thanks to the access to computer facilities.

Social facilities and amenities and economic activities need to be analysed as an exercise in locational analysis. It is in this area that geographers have used so far the application of Central Places and Growth Centres, but these have been 'foot loose' because the resources and their levels of utilisation influencing the pattern of emergence of nodes or central places have hardly been considered in a spatial context.

Emphasis on environment, programmes to alleviate poverty conditions (National Rural Employment Programme, IRDP (Integrated Rural Development Pragramme) intended to create durable assets) and several *ad hoc* plan programmes (e.g. SFDA, Small Farmer Development Agency) need to be inbuilt in our studies in Integrated Area Planning lest they degenerate to the situation where they can neither be treated as micro-regional studies nor as exercises oriented to planning.

The concept of Integrated Area Development lays stress on *spatial integration of* development activities. This aspect has been lacking in the procedure adopted in the planning process at all the levels of the political-administrative framework, namely the national, state and District levels. The approach to *spatial integration* itself has often been spelt out and practiced differently by specialists from different social sciences and also the planners and administrators. The approach to spatial integration should be attempted at different scale of the geographical surface ranging from the micro (comparable to the size of a District and below) to macro (group of states or parts thereof) levels with appropriate levels of aggregation or dis-aggregation of activities according to their relative importance. At the micro level the geographic space provides a spatial framework which is realistic. At this level all the human settlements can be plotted on a map and their spatial patterns of distribution, linkages, social services and facilities and economic activities and their interrelationship can be studied as a part of the evolution of the region as a functional-economic entity. Likewise, the resource base - particularly of agriculture, forestry, minerals, water and power can be evaluated in terms of their area coverage in the geographical surface. In fact, the strategy for integrated area development implies integration of human settlements population and its attributes included with the resource base; and the necessary conditions are provided by the spatial framework mentioned above.

It is against this background of the conceptual framework that the present study is an attempt to highlight the spatial aspects of the strategy for integrated Area Development.

A good deal of confusion also exists in the Planning literature in India regarding micro-level planning, Area Development, Integrated Rural Development and so on. The present study in its spatial view regards the twin facets of rural and urban aspects of development as interrelated. Viewed from this consideration the urban centres and a large number of rural settlements are to be treated as "nodes" which are necessary for integrated development of the areas at the level of Development Block (village clusters) and the District, village being the lowest or local unit of planning.

NOTES

1. Government of India, Planning Commission (1953) : *The First Five Year Plan* pp. 128-143.

2. Bhat, L.S. with Rao, V.L.S.P. (1960): *Planning Regions in the Mysore State - the*

Need for Re-adjustment of District Boundaries, Indian Statistical Institute, Calcutta.

3. Government of India, Planning Commission (1961) : *Third Five Year Plan* pp. 142-154.

4. Government of India (1961) : *Third Five Year Plan* pp. 142-154 Planning Commission.

5. Bhat, L.S. *et al* (1976) : *Micro-level Planning - A Case Study of Karnal Area*, K.B. Publications, New Delhi.

6. Losch, A. (1954) : *The Economics of Location* Yale University Press, New Haven.

Isard, W. (1956) : *Location and Space Economy*, John Wiley & Sons, New York.

Haggett, P. *et.al* (1979) : *Locational analysis in Human Geography* Edward Arnold, London.

Rao, V.L.S.P. (1963) : *Regional Planning*, Indian Statistical Institute, Calcutta.

7. Geddes, P. (1940) : *Cities in Evolution* Williams and Norgate.

8. A number of studies in the Identification of Growth Centres were started early in 1970s.

Government of India, Ministry of Food and Agriculture (1973) : *The Pilot Research Project in Growth centres* : A Ford Foundation Staff Document.

9. Bhat, L.S. (1972) : *Regional Planning in India*, Statistical Publishing Society, Calcutta.

10. At the higher level in the political administrative hierarchy, Zones comprising groups of States have to be created with the aim of economic integration of States and sub-regions.

TWO

The Study Area - North Kanara District

North Kanara District[1] is one of the 19 Districts of Karnataka. Bounded by the Arabian sea to its west it forms the Northern coastal District of Karnataka with South Kanara District as its counterpart both together comprising the coastal sub-region of the State. The District is contiguous with Goa to its north. Prior to the merger of Goa with the Indian Union in December 1961 its socio-economic interaction with the Konkan coast as sub-region of Maharashtra, and in particular with Bombay was via the peninsular plateau route passing through Hubli and Pune (Fig. 2).

The District has a total area of 10,291 km^2(average size of the District in Karnataka is 10,093 km^2) and a population of 1,072 034 persons dwelling in 1283 rural settlements and 13 towns. Of the total population, 25 percent is urban; the corresponding percentage for the State is 25.35. If the towns irrespective of population size and functions are considered as the nodal centres for spatial integration of the Districts' economy one town serves 792 km^2. Though the level of urbanisation measured by the percentage of people living in towns is almost equal to that of the State and India, the urban centres are mostly service centres having been the Headquarters of the Tahsils and the District. Of the 13 towns 5 are of class III (20000-50000 persons) category, 6 are class IV towns (10000-20000 persons), and one each of class V and VI category (5000-10000 and less than 5000 persons respectively). It can thus be seen that the District has a highly imbalanced urban structure with a very weak pattern of nodality required for integrated development of the area.

The population density per Km^2 of the District has been the lowest in Karnataka both in 1971 (83 person km^2) and 1981 (104 persons km^2) on account of rugged topography. Nearly 75 percent of the total area is hilly and rugged and the coastal plain (unlike in South Kanara District) is very narrow (less than 2 kms in most parts) and indented by the west flowing rivers and the spurs of the Western Ghats abutting the coast. Nearly 44 percent of the rural population lives in villages of less than 1000 population and 65 percent of the villages are of less than 500 persons. Growth-rate of population during 1971-81 was + 26.25 (State average +26.75). From continuously negative rate of growth until 1921 (1911-21 growth rate - 6.69 per cent) growth-rate of population started showing low positive value (+4.01 percent during 1921-31); and it is only during 1951-61 that the growth-rate exceeded that of the State average (+21.57 percent).[2] This has been attributed partly to immigration of people from the coastal areas who till recently were seasonal migrants to work in garden lands devoted to spices and fruits. Secondly, mortality has considerably declined with the eradication of malaria.

Sex ratio is 958 (962 for the State), and it is generally low in the *Malnad* area (916) due to marriage migration of females to areas outside the region a feature so common in recent times because of the preference of relatively better off households having garden crops to arrange marriage of their daughters with educated employed males in bigger cities. Sex ratio for the coastal area is high - an indication of out migration of males to large cities like Bangalore and Bombay. This pattern of migration is characteristic of the entire west coast region.

Contrary to the conditions prevailing in other parts of the State and India, even though the District remained under developed literacy has been high (57.35 percent as against 48.81 percent for the State). This is attributed to better facilities for education provided by the erstwhile Bombay province of which the District was a part and the impact of Bombay which attracted a large number of job seekers prior to Re-organisation of the States in 1956.[3] This trend has continued even now.

The resource base of the District comprises mainly its forests, plantation crops (arecanut, pepper, cardamom , co-conut and a variety of fruits). Nearly 81 percent of the total area of the District is under forest of which teak wood has been by far the predominant and famous one commanding a large market upto Bombay and

Banglore. Because of heavy rainfall and the rugged terrain of the Western Ghats and its transverse ranges, the forests are extensive occupying areas above 50-75 metres from the sea level. These are mostly deciduous with strands of evergreen trees; and where the flat lands occur away from streams there are some grass lands. These are often lateritic uplands and slopes. Sandalwood trees are also common particularly in the drier and more open areas in the eastern part of the District.

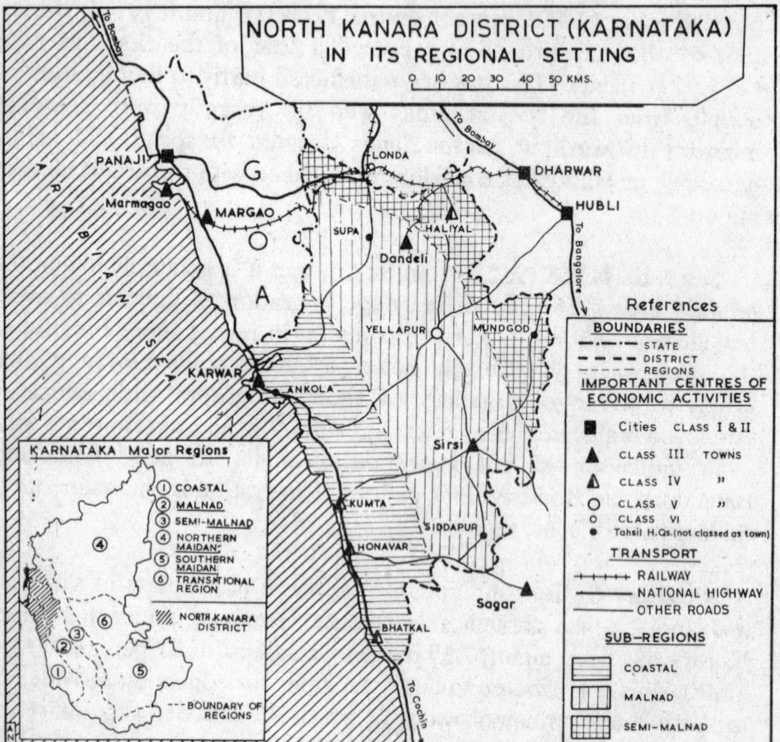

Fig. 2

Cultivated area is only 10 percent of the total area of the District of which only 11 percent is sown more than once while the areas under plantations are perennial. Double cropped areas are restricted to coastal plains of mostly paddy during the kharif season while groundnut and pulses are cultivated in the winter months taking advantage of the available moisture after the rains which last until

October. Fallows and culturable wastes occupy about 3 percent of the total area. On the whole, there is very little scope for increasing the cultivated area while with increased deforestation the problems of erosion and availability of green leaves for plantation crops are becoming acute. Spatial arrangement and structure of land use and cropping pattern under topographical and climatic constraints are strongly suggestive of the need for integration of land uses on an ecological - economic considerations.

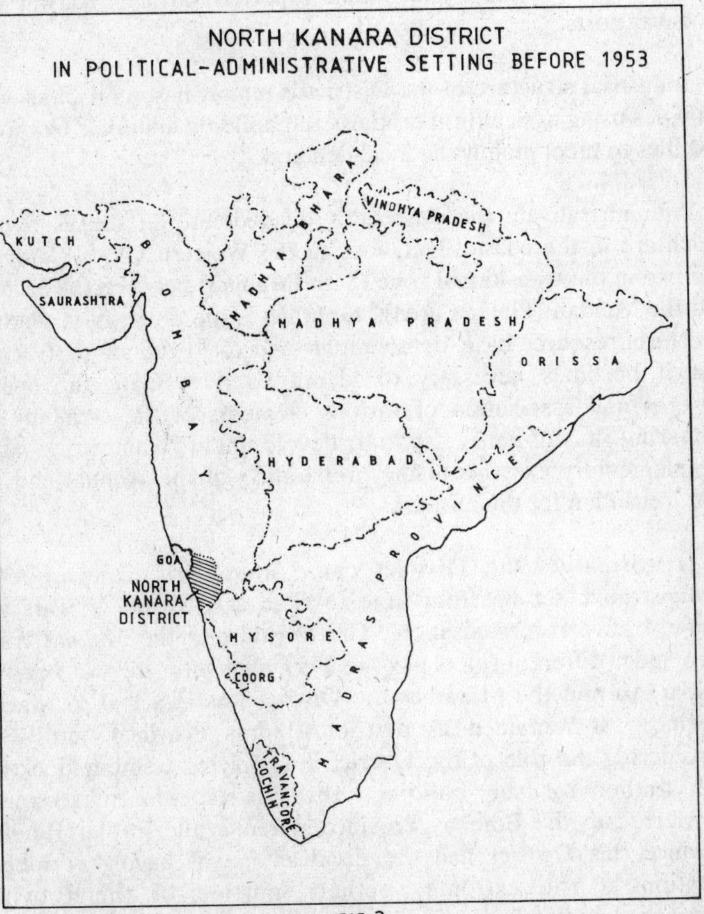

FIG. 3

Apart from forestry and agriculture, the District is endowed with fishery (both inland and sea-fishing) on account of the large coast line of about 160 kms and rivers of which the Kali and the Sharawati are important from the point of view of hydro-electricity production. The Kali Hydro-electric Project now under construction is going to be the biggest power generating unit in the country.

Among the minerals iron ore, manganese, limestone and bauxite are important. Manganese ore is mined mainly is Supa area in the northern part of the Malnad and exported through Karwar and Honavar ports.

Industrial structure of the District is mainly based on small scale activities using agricultural produce and building materials like wood and tiles to meet mainly the local demand.

Administratively the District is divided into 11 tahsils five of which are in the coastal belt, four in the Western Ghats *(Malnad)* and two in the transitional zone (Semi-Malnad) between the *Malnad* and the Maidan (Plateau area).[4] So much is the diversity in physical structure, resource base, demographic and socio-economic structure that it becomes necessary to identify and evaluate the spatial patterns and association of various elements of the economy for preparing a *normative* spatial development framework as a complementary exercise in the preparation of the Annual and the Five Year Plan for the District.

Historically, the District came under different political administrative set up from time to time as a result of wars and administrative re-organisation. The coastal and the *Malnad* tracts were under different rulers prior to 1799 when after the war between Haidar Ali and the Marathas the District was attached to Madras Province. It remained as part of Madras Province until 1865. Considering the role of the District in supplying Bombay dockyard with timber for ship-building, the District was subsequently transferred to the Bombay Province. Even in the former Bombay Province this District had the disadvantage of having peripheral situation at the extreme southern portion of the Province sandwiched between Goa as the Portuguese Territory and South Kanara District as part of the Madras Province (Fig. 3). State and international boundaries imposed artificial barriers of different magnitude for inter dependent economic development. The colonial administration provided Bombay all the advantages to emerge as the major port for the export of raw materials from its hinterland and to receive all the benefits accruing from it. The second role of the District was one of acting as a corridor for the export of cotton grown in the adjoining *Desh* tract (Peninsular Plateau area of black soil) through its small ports such as Kumta, or as supplier of primary forest and plantation products to meet the demands outside the District.[5] Internally, the spatial arrangement and of socio-economic interaction among the human settlements was marked by sharp discontinuities both in the coastal and the *Malnad* tracts of the District due to the dictates of environment and lack of development perspectives. Almost all the rivers were unbridged causing interruption in the movement of goods and people within the District and the rest of the area with which the District could interact as it has been happening now. With the extension of the railway line from Bombay to Hubli the District lost even the corridor situation resulting in the stagnation of port towns like Karwar, Kumta, Honavar and Bhatkal in the coastal area and the decline of Sirsi, Siddapur and Yellapur in the Malnad area which acted till then as transit centres between the coastal area and the peninsular Plateau. Until the 1940s the Malnad was known more for malaria and tales of food poisoning and other social evils than the forestry and planatation economy which contribute substantially to the District and State income.

At different times in the historical past North Kanara District has been sighted as a prosperous area. This prosperity was mainly on account of the trade through its ports. The exports were mainly rice, coconut, pepper and spices, palm sugar and iron ore.[6] Even today these are the principal produce of the area. Besides, the ports handled commodies like cotton from the interior Desh tract because of the absence of railways connecting Hubli and Marmagoa with Bombay. Arabs and Persian travellers during the 13th century mentioned Chitakul, Bhatkal and Honavar as prosperous ports.

It is this prosperity of the area and the port facility which attracted in the 18th century the Portuguese and British enterprises to locate their establishments. The invasion by Maratha and Mysore rulers on the Portuguese and English factories led to long strife and unstable political conditions; and the development of Bombay and growth of railways relegated the area to its under development from early 18th century. The ports started silting up and the policy of the erstwhile Bombay Province to bring more area under forest and the decline of population due to malaria and other diseases led to the decline of area under plantation crops particularly of pepper and arecanut.[7]

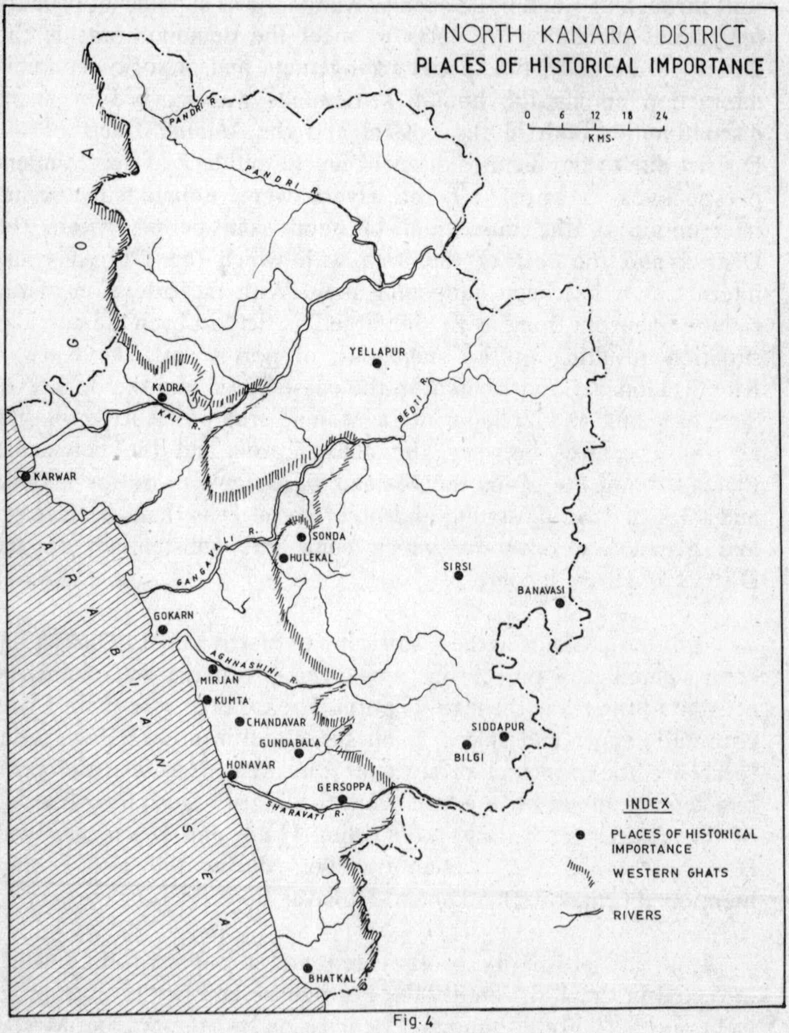

Fig. 4

There are also evidence of inland trading centres such as Kadra. Gundabala, Mirjan, Chandavar and Gersoppa taking advantage of navigability of rivers upto about 32 kms from the mouth of the river (Fig. 4).[8]

Other locations which acted as centres of religious and cultural contacts are Gokarn in the coastal tract famous for the Shiva temple, Sonda, Banavasi and Hulekal in the Malnad tract which were the seat of Jain Chieftans and of trade in local produce.[9] Another settlement - Bilgi in the Malnad was the seat of the Vijayanagar empire. All these centres are now small villages with imprints of the past glory. The towns like Yellapur, Sirsi and Siddapur were mere transit centres situated close to the edge of the Western Ghats.

Re-organisation of States in 1956 brought about a marked reversal in the orientation of the District's economy from Bombay inwards into the enlarged Mysore State (re-named Karnataka). The economy of the District had to undergo considerable stresses and strains particularly in trading of commercial crops and competition with relatively developed towns situated outside the District e.g. Mangalore in the South Kanara District, Panaji and Marmagoa in the north (now a Union Territory after liberation in 1961), Hubli to the east and Shimoga to the south-east. It is pertinent to observe that over the years these places have grown as strong regional economic centres outside the District and their linkages with every important rural and urban centre of the North Kanara District has strengthened the centrifugal forces of economic development, in that the District can not hope to develop in the years to come strong backward and forward linkages between the resources and economic activities so vital for integrated development. On the contrary, development of transport routes without complementary socio-economic inputs have brought important areas of commercial crops and trading centres into the fold of above mentioned centres only to subserve and not to emerge as centres of growth of the District's economy.[10] The newly constructed West Coast Highway connecting Bombay with KanyaKumari through Panaji in Goa and Mangalore in South Kanara District serves to re-orient the economic links of the coastal towns of this District with these more developed port towns.

NOTES

1. Name of the district was changed to *Uttara Kannada* District by Government of Karnataka notification in 1977. Similarly the coastal District of South Kanara was changed to Dakshina Kanada District. The original name is used in this study as it is more familiar for references in Atlases, reports and Census Records prior to 1977.

2. In fact the entire area of the *Malnad* (Western Ghats sub-region in Karnataka of rugged hills, per humid climate forests and in accessibility) had experienced decline in population due to high mortality rate until 1921 and rapid increase since 1951 e.g., Chikmagalur District (+ 43.03), Shimoga (+ 53.38), Coorg (+ 40.72).

3. Deshpande, C.D. *et. al* (1980) : Impact of a *Metropolitan City on the Surrounding Region - A Study of South Colaba, Maharashtra*, Concept Publishing Company, New Delhi.

4. The North Kanara District is the only District in Karnataka which has parts of the three sub-regions of Karnataka which extend longitudinally. Ref : Learmonth A.T.A. and Bhat L.S. (1958) : *Mysore State - Vol. I - Atlas of Resources* and Learmonth A.T.A. *et. al* (1980) : *Mysore State - Vol. II - A Regional Synthesis.* Indian Statistical Institute and Asia Publishing House, Bombay.

5. Cotton exported from Kumta port had acquired the name "Kumta Cotton".

6. Silva, S. (1957) : *Malnad* or *Male Nadu* : All India Malnad Third conference, Sirsi.

7. This is perhaps one of the explanations for the occurrence of irrigation channels and abandoned house sites deep in the forest areas of the Malnand.

8. Kadra is located about 32 kms upstream from the port town Karwar at the mouth of the Kali River; Gundabala is located about 24 kms upstream from the Gangavali river mouth; Mirjan about 12 kms upstream from the Aghanashini river mouth and Gersoppa about 27 kms from Honavar port along the river Sharavati.

9. Banavasi was also the focal point for the central part of the Malnad through which all the trade routes from the Plateau area to the ports passed.

10. This is evident in the case of the coastal sub-region of the Maharashtra (Konkan coastal region) sandwiched between the developed areas like Goa and Bombay at the extremisties.

THREE

Physical Setting

Topography has introduced marked contrasts within the District in respect of the spatial arrangement, areal extent, type and quality of the resource base. In the previous chapter the analysis of the situation and historical factors that have left an imprint on the geographical personality of the District serves to focus on the future strategy for development in spatial terms. To a large extent topography, situation and historical factors are interrelated and have combined influence on the development processes and patterns.

First of all, the configuration of the macro relief features of the West coast region, the Western Ghats and the Peninsular Plateau of which the North Kanara District possesses parts of each need to be characterised with a view to evaluate the importance of topography on other features of the District's economy (Fig. 4). The coastal sub-region of Karnataka comprising parts of the North Kanara and South Kanara District is itself transitional in many respects between the Konkan coast (of Maharashtra and of Goa)and the coastal sub-region of Kerala. Whereas the Konkan coastal sub-region has all the characteristics of the Deccan Lava land forms with flat topped and steep sided residual hills emanating from the scarpline of the Western Ghats and dissected narrow coastal plain, the coastal sub-region of Karnataka is made of Archaean gneisses and granite hills capped by laterites owing to high rainfall. The narrow valleys of short stretched rivers flowing into the Arabian sea have fertile alluvial soil; and these narrow valleys culminate in the development of elongated coastal plains of sand and aluvium. Where the tributary streams coalesce they form alluvial tracts which are relatively wider. Here again the distinction between the coastal tracts of North Kanara and South Kanara are noteworthy in that the coastal plains are much wider in South Kanara than those in North Kanara.

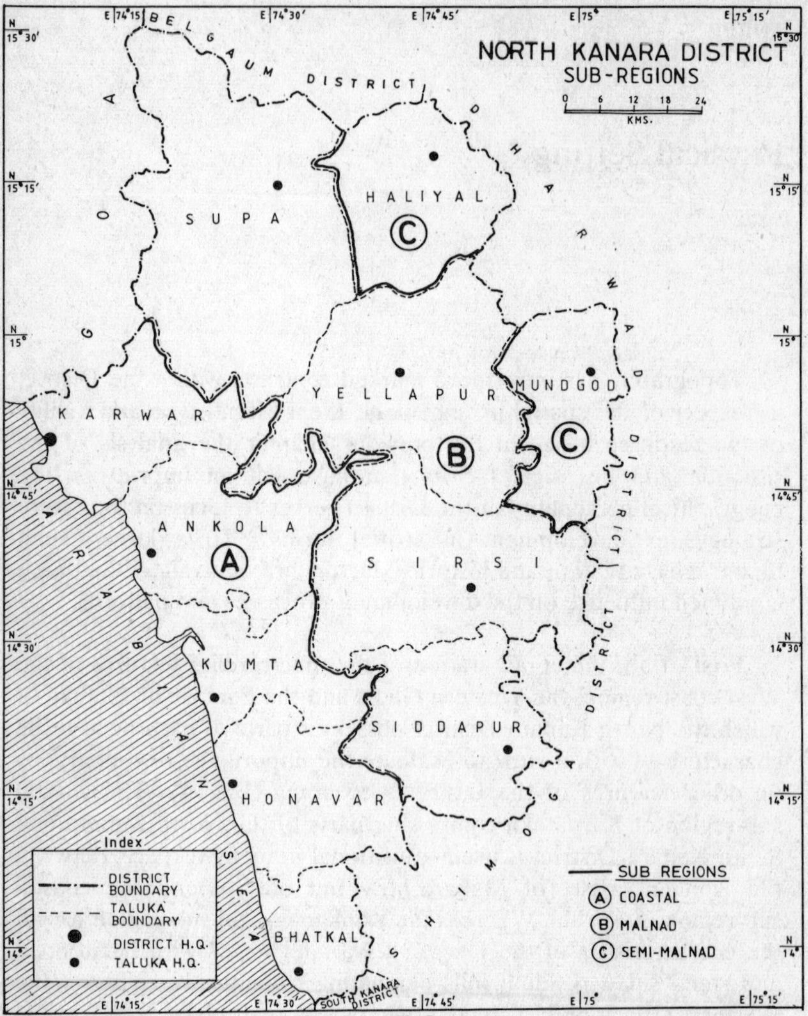

Fig. 5

1. **Coastal tract**: (Fig.5) There is nothing like a coastal plain in North Kanara; and its features are that of a coastline of sub-megence with the scrapline of Western Ghats representing the faulted edge and a number of islands off the coastal area into the sea showing evidences of sub-mergence of the land mass. In between are the plain areas formed by sand dunes and silt brought down by the rivers. These areas are nowhere more than 1 to 4 kms wide and the

foot hills form a distinct tract with residual hills and narrow valleys. The important rivers that originate from Western Ghats flowing into the Arabian sea are, from North to South - the Kalinadi, Gangavali-Bedti, Aghanashini and the Sharavati and each river is marked by a water fall as it leaves the scarpline of the Western Ghats, the famous one being the Joga Falls on the Sharvati river.

The width of the coastal tract upto the scarpline of the Western Ghats is approximately 32 kms; and most of it forms the foot hill area of the Western Ghats with narrow valleys and relatively flat alluvial patches at the confluence of the tributary stream with the main rivers. These are separated by lateritic hills often rising to 500 metres to 600 metres above sea level. The scarp edge of the Western Ghats itself is of lower height (approximately 700 metres) in this part in comparison with its counter part in Maharashtra and southern part of Karnataka (e.g. Kudremukh 1892 metres, Brahmagiri near Mercara in Coorg 1355 metres). Thus the coastal tract comprises two distinct sub-divisions (i) The narrow indented coastal plain and (ii) the relatively wide foot hill area extending upto the scarpline of the Western Ghats.

2. **The Western Ghats**: Because of the extensively humid forests the Western Ghats region in Karnataka is known as the *Malnad*. Unlike in the South Kanara District the Western Ghats forms a distinct sub-region stretching North-South in the centre of the District. In its width this tract varies from 30 kms to 45 kms on account of differential headward erosion by the major rivers and their tributaries. In places, as that of the Joga Falls on the Sharavati river the headward erosion from the original faulted edge of the Western Ghats to the present position of the water fall is upto about 18 kms.

These characteristics have resulted in the occurrence of river captures in many places. The most prominent one is of the Pandri river now a tributary of the Kali river. The Pandri river flows in a NW-SE direction in Supa Taluka for over 65 kms and then takes a swift westerly turn to join the Kali river. Such features of river capture and headward erosion of tributary streams have led to the formation of deep gullies and cutting of river banks resulting in depletion of water to the spice gardens for which the Malnad area of North Kanara is famous.

From the edge of the Ghats upto about 16 kms the Malnad

presents a picture of rugged hills rising higher eastward and then the topography is one of flat or gently sloping land. There is however a marked difference in the topography between the northern part of the Malnad mainly in Supa taluka where the hills are higher and have steep slopes; as such the tract appears more rugged. The southern part in Yellapur, Sirsi and Siddapur talukas is relatively flat and undulating with superficial perennial streams that are an advantage to spice and plantation crops.

3. The Semi-Malnad

This is a transitional tract between the Maland and the *Maidan* (Plateau). Everything is truly transitional. It tends to be an open country occasionally intercepted by residual hills. The vegetation itself reflects the transition from the deciduous and evergreen forest types to stunted bushes and scrubs. Such landforms and land use are typical of the eastern parts of Haliyal and Mundgod tabukas. The administrative boundaries of these talukas do not reveal the narrow and contiguous tract of the Semi-Malnad which is distinguishable on large scale maps of landform and land use. The Semi-Malnad tract for Karnataka as a whole and its characteristics are vividly broughtout in an earlier study.[1]

Physical Landscape - Sub-regions

The above analysis of the physical landscape has served to identify the following sub-divisions of North Kanara based on the physical characteristics.

TABLE 1: Sub-regions of North Kanara District

Sub-Regions	Administrative Units comprising Part or whole of the Talukas
1.The coastal tract	
i. The coastal plain proper	Karwar, Ankola, Kumta, Honavar, Bhatkal.
ii. The foot hills	eastern part of the above talukas.
2.The Western Ghats (Malnad)	
i. Northern	Supa and parts of Yellapur and Haliyal
ii. Southern	Yellapur, Sirsi, Siddapur
3.Semi Malnad	Haliyal, Mundgod

Groups of talukas comprising these sub-regions are used for the analysis of spatial patterns and variations of the resource base. In the case of human resources' settlements as locations along with their attributes are used in the analysis along with the aggregated values at the sub-regional levels.

NOTES

1. Learmonth A.T.A. and Bhat L.S. (1960) : *Mysore State Vol. I. Atlas of Resources* Indian Statistical Institute and Asia Publishing House, Bombay, pp. 16-32 and Rao, V.L.S.P. and Bhat, L.S. (1960) : *Planning Regions in the Mysore State* Indian Statistical Institute, Calcutta.

FOUR

Resource Base

The physical setting analysed in the foregoing pages serves to provide insight into the nature of the resources their spatial pattern of distribution and the patterns and problems of development arising out of the characteristics and configuration of the physical landscape. First of all it is the limited extent of land available for cultivation and its spatial arrangement that explains the variations in the overall low density of population and the distribution of settlements. They are linear along the coastal sand dunes and allival plains and girdling along the junction of the hills and the plains in the coastal sub-region. In the Malnand they are linear closely following the narrow stream valleys. There are isolated hamlets scattered in the forested hills and relatively nucleated settlements in the Semi Malnad. Forests dominate the land use of the District covering nearly 81 per cent of the total geographical area and these occupy most of the area beyond 75 meter contour from the coastal plain. About 8 percent of the total area includes uncultivable land, fallows, pastures and other miscellaneous uses; and the remaining portion of the land is cultivated.

1. **Agricultural Land Use** (Table 2 and Fig. 6) : Cultivated area is mostly below 1° - 2° slope. It is contiguous and extensive in the coastal plains and the Semi-Malnad while it is patchy or occurs in narrow belts along the tuibutary valleys in the coastal foot hills and the Malnad area. Of the net area sown, 38 percent of it occurs in coastal tract, 35 percent in the Malnad and 27 percent in the Semi-Malnad. Within the limited extent of cultivated area in the District there are distinct spatial variations reflecting the influence of topography.

TABLE 2: North Kanara District--Spatial Variations in Landuse (1983-84) (percent to total geographical area).

Taluka	Sub-region	Forest	Barren & uncul tivable land	Land put to non-agri. use	Perman-ent pa-stures	Land under misc. tree crops	Current fallow	Other fall-ows	Culti-vable waste	Net area sown	Area sown more than once
	COASTAL	76.00	2.78	3.10	1.94	0.99	0.56	0.87	1.27	12.43	13.56
Karwar	"	75.72	6.14	0.52	0.16	0.51	1.11	1.40	0.74	13.70	4.94
Ankola	"	82.33	1.97	1.73	1.49	0.84	0.36	1.13	1.22	8.90	9.77
Kumta	"	68.64	3.85	4.99	4.15	-	0.62	0.25	1.65	16.44	12.40
Honavar	"	76.36	0.25	6.04	1.72	1.80	0.42	0.66	1.57	11.18	22.32
Bhatkal	"	73.00	1.54	2.58	3.69	2.28	0.11	0.55	1.22	15.02	25.82
	MALNAD	87.00	1.39	0.73	2.32	0.08	0.17	0.73	0.80	7.02	9.27
Supa	"	93.19	0.36	1.44	0.07	-	0.11	0.92	0.63	3.28	5.57
Yellapur	"	90.86	1.26	0.05	0.92	0.04	0.21	0.22	0.78	5.67	6.17
Sirsi	"	78.87	2.85	0.24	5.66	0.29	0.29	0.55	1.01	10.75	10.42
Siddapur	"	79.32	1.60	0.97	4.24	0.02	0.04	1.37	0.87	11.57	12.87
	SEMI-MALNAD	72.00	2.74	0.51	0.46	0.75	0.71	2.31	1.65	19.15	9.79
Haliyal	"	69.98	8.14	0.56	0.82	0.90	0.42	1.82	1.15	21.20	4.06
Mundgod	"	73.94	2.23	0.45		0.55	1.08	2.93	2.20	16.53	11.10
District		81.00	2.00	1.50	1.90	0.50	0.40	1.00	1.10	10.60	11.08

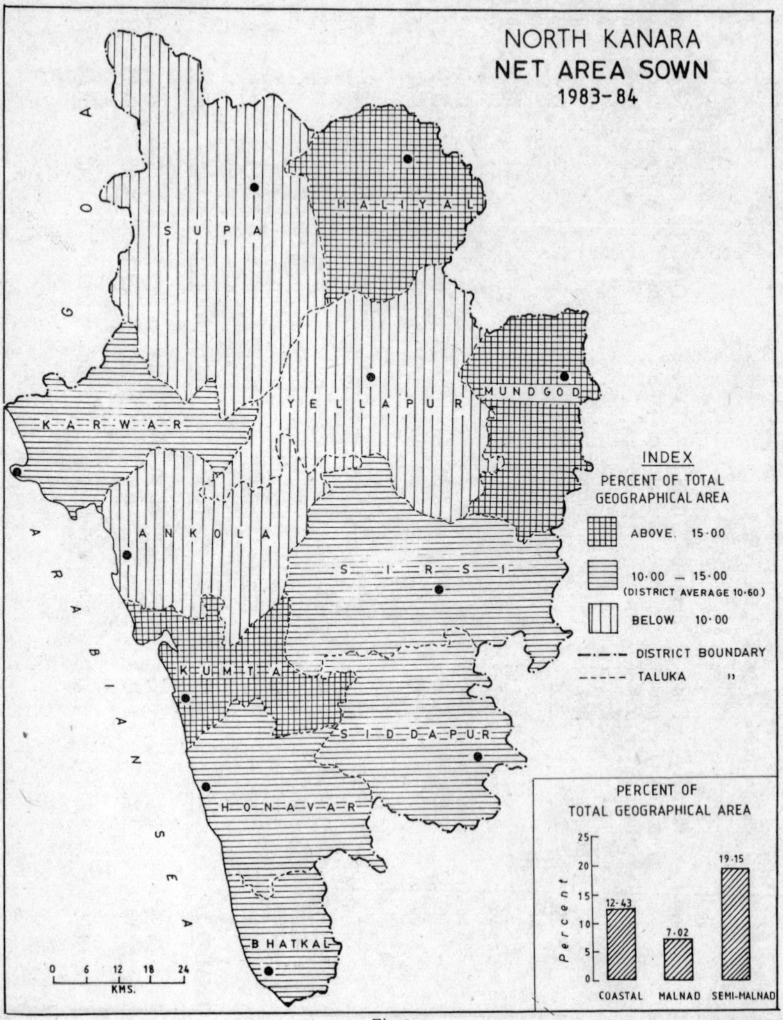

Fig·6

For example, in the coastal tract (including foot hills) it is 12.4 percent of the total geographical area, 7 percent in the Malnad and 19 percent in the Semi-Malnad. In each of these zones problems and potentialities for upgrading the land quality and land use are different and require specific strategy. For example, in the coastal tract there is the problem of salinity and water logging in the plains - particularly at the mouth of the river leading to the formation of marshy land. Likewise, the windblown sand deposition, formation of sand bars parallel to the coast and the need for afforestation of the barren sand dunes are specific problems requiring area approach. Similarly, cultivation of paddy in the low-lying sandy and alluvial plain and irrigation of coconut gardens need integrated planning of tank and well irrigation. Likewise, in the coastal foot hill area the problems of soil erosion, lateritisation of top layers of rocks, afforestation, horticulture and cultivation of fodder crops for feeding the cattle in the plains are the priorities in planning.

In the Malnad area, the approach to integrated land use is in relation to the interdependence of spice gardens and the adjoining woodlands (locally known as *betta* lands). This is because one acre of spice garden requires atleast two acres of woodland for the supply of green leaf manure. With increased felling of trees, the spice gardens are deprived of the input of greenleaf manure. Reserve forests situated close to these lands are as such encroached resulting in degradation of the forest wealth.

Another aspect related to integrated resource development is in respect of the use of water resources of the area for major hydro-electricity projects. The Sharavati and the Kali River projects have already inundated large tracts of valuable forest areas and the proposed Bedti River Power Project in Sirsi-Siddapur area is a threat to about 10 percent of the Reserve Forests in this tract.

In the Semi-Malnad the cultivated area is mostly in contiguous tracts interspersed with open forests or wood lands.

1.1. **Cropping Pattern** (Table No. 3)

Paddy is predominant in the cropping pattern and is grown mostly as a kharif crop taking advantage of assured rainfall. Next in importance are the garden crops which occupy 16 percent of the cropped area contributing to about 40 percent of the District income. These crops include co-conut, cardamom, pepper, betetnut and a variety of fruits among which cashew, jack fruit, banana and pineapple are important. Sugar cane is grown only in 2 percent of the cultivated area taking advantage of perennial streams; and is used mostly for local consumption after processing as jaggery.

Likewise, ragi as a millet is grown in the drier foot hill areas, and other millets (mainly jowar) in the drier portion in the Semi-Malnad. They occupy only about 2 percent of the total cropped area. Intensity of cultivation measured by the extent of irrigation and area sown more than once is only 11 percent.

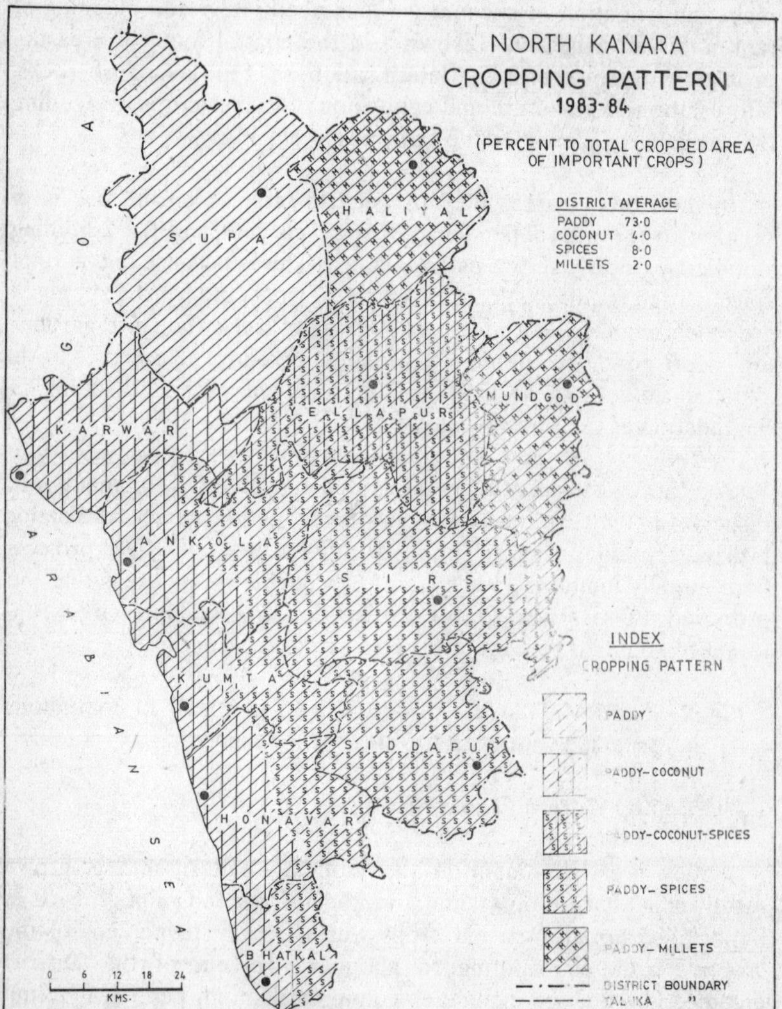

Fig. 7

TABLE 3: North Kanara District--cropping Pattern (1983-84) (Figures in percent to total cropped area)*

Taluka	Sub-region	Paddy	Ragi	Other Millets (Jowar)	Pulses	Ground nut	Coco-nut	Sugar Cane	Fruits and Veg-etables	Spices
COASTAL										
Karwar	"	83	-	-	-	1	7	1	6	-
Ankola	"	73	-	-	-	6	7	2	8	3
Kumta	"	71	-	-	-	5	9	2	7	4
Honavar	"	56	-	-	-	7	14	4	6	7
Bhatkal	"	69	-	-	-	7	7	2	5	3
MALNAD										
Supa	"	90	1	-	-	-	1	2	3	1
Yellapur	"	73	-	-	-	-	4	2	5	15
Sirsi	"	68	1	-	-	-	1	4	4	20
Siddapur	"	62	-	-	-	-	-	1	5	26
SEMI-MALNAD										
Haliyal	"	81	1	2	1	-	-	2	1	-
Mundgod	"	78	1	7	-	-	-	-	1	-
District		73	1	1	-	2	4	2	4	8

* Only important crops are included

Spatial affinity of crops within the District is quite distinct in that paddy is cultivated extensively (in terms of area) in the coastal plains though in terms of the percentage of area, paddy dominates in almost all the sub-regions. Nearly 38 percent of the area under paddy of the District is in the coastal tract, 34 percent in the Malnad area and 28 percent in the Semi-Malnad. Intra-regional variations are however quite revealing reflecting the impact of topography and soils. Where the coastal plains are narrow and the foot hill interiors have large number of tributary stream valleys, paddy gives way to garden crops resembling the cropping pattern of the Malnad. For example, Honavar taluka has only 56 percent of the cultivated area under paddy and 7 percent of the cultivated area is under spice gardens.

In contrast, in the area of lateritic slopes and table land, as in Bhatkal taluka, the area under paddy is only 69 percent. Spice gardens are less (occupying only 3 percent of the cultivated area). In the remaining parts of the coastal area percentage of paddy land varies from 71 percent in Kumta taluka to 83 percent in Karwar taluka. Co-conut gardens are significant mostly in coastal sandy belt and are reared around human dwellings. They occupy 7 to 14 percent of the total cultivated area in the coastal tract while it decreases to about 1 to 4 percent in the Malnad area. The coconut gardens around human dwellings are replaced by spice gardens in the Malnad area. The predominant spice and horticulture areas of Sirsi, Siddapur and Yellapur talukas have 15 to 26 percent of the cultivated area under these crops. Here again, Supa taluka in northern area is insignificant in most of the garden crops (spices and co-conut have only 1 percent each of the cultivated area). This explains the impact of more hilly and rugged topography in the area where the tributary streams of the Kali river provide all signs of river captures and resultant headward erosion of the streams close to the Western Ghat's edge.

In the Semi-Malnad area, while paddy dominates, cultivation of millets (of which jawar is important) is an indication of the transition from the wet forested hill tract to the relatively drier more open country of the Peninsular Plateau (Northern Maidan of Karnataka).

Since paddy is mostly a kharif crop, parts of these lands mostly in the coastal plains and the semi-Malnad are devoted to pulses and oil seeds of which groundnut is now becoming increasingly important as a cash crop.

2. Forests

The major resource of this District is forest wealth with all the topographic and climatic condition being favourable. In fact 65 percent of the forest produce in the form of valuable timber and other produce of Karnataka is contributed by this District. Teak, rosewood and bamboo are the important varieties of trees that are grown here. Besides, they also provide sandalwood, matches, resins and a variety of medicinal herbs. Small scale industries of the District based on these materials are an important part of the District's economy.

The forest cover is however relegated to steep slopes of the Western Ghats and inaccessible areas on account of large scale exploitation. The secondary data available on taluka basis bring out significant intra-District variations (Table 2). While the District as a whole has 81 percent of the total geographical area under forest it is as low as 68 percent in the coastal area around Kumta where the lateritic uplands have little vegetal cover. Likewise, in the more open tract around Haliyal in Semi-Malnad forests occupy 70 percent of the total geographical area. These areas have rainfall of only about 140 cms, and as such, the forests differ both in quality and areal spread.

In the coastal tract the percentage of area under forest is 76; in the Malnad it is 87 percent while in Semi-Malnad it is 72 percent. Within these tracts the data reveal further significant variations. For example, in the Malnad around Supa and yellapur the area under forest is 91 to 93 percent.

Development of forest resources in the District needs spatial approach as the forest cover varies very closely with topographical conditions; and the forest land use is closely linked with agriculture as explained elsewhere. Likewise, there is need to classify forest areas by type and levels of importance (local, regional, State and National). A prerequisite for this purpose is an up-to-date inventory of forest resources in the form of spatial coverage revealed through large scale maps and satellite imageries on a scale of 1:50 000 and 1:250 000 so that the aspects of integration of related land use can be evaluated in their ecological setting.

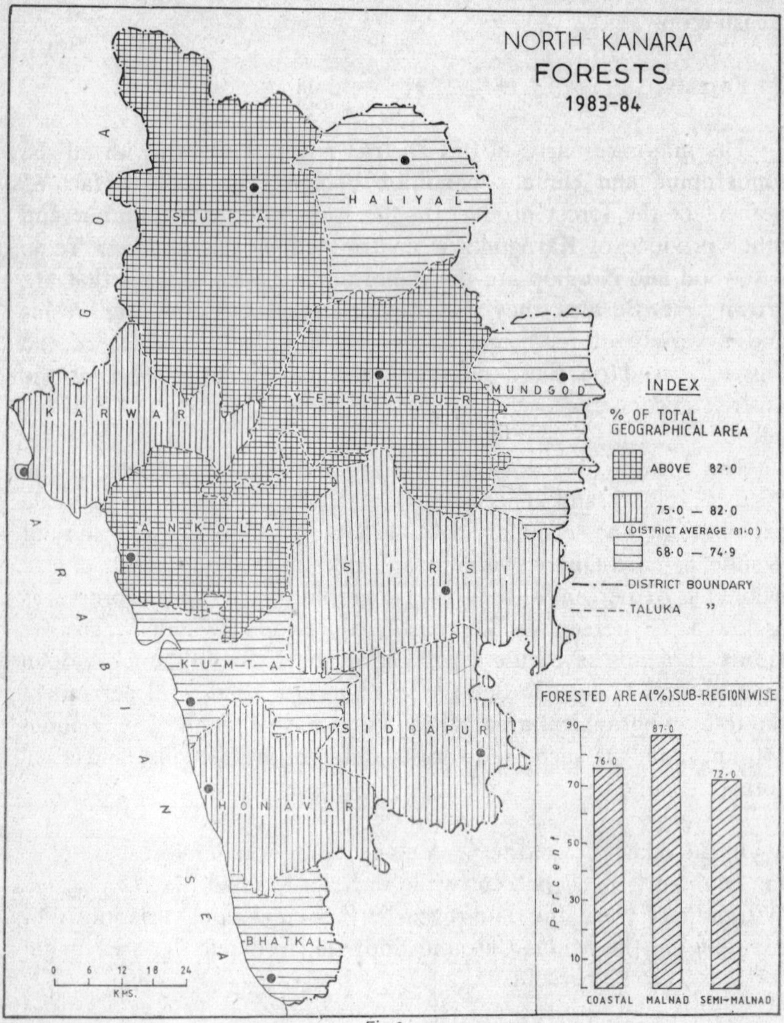

Fig-8

3. Minerals

By far the District's mineral resources so far exploited include Manganese ore associated with Dharwar Schistose rocks in Supa Taluka of the Northern Malnad. This area alone contributes to 65 percent of the total output. The ore is transported by road to the port town of Karwar for export. About 200,00 tonnes of Manganese ore are presently exploited. Low grade iron ore also occurs in the lateritic hills in the coastal foot-hill area around Karwar, Kumta and Honavar. Limestone occurs in the central part of Malnad around Yellapur. Some bauxite associated with laterites is yet to be exploited.

Granite and laterites are also quarried for use mainly as building materials. Lime-shells upto about 13,000 tonnes were produced in coastal tracts in 1980-81. Clay from lateritic soils are mostly used for tile making. In the coastal area, salt is produced taking advantage of inundation of land by saline water during high tide. These salt pans are mostly found near Kumta.

4. Fishery

With a long coastline and inland water bodies fishery is important in the development of the District awaiting large scale exploitation. The major fishing centres are Honavar, Tadri and Karwar although all along the shoreline the fishing communities look to the sea for their means of livelihood. With the location of a number of ice factories and salt production it has become possible to expand the development of fishery for export of fish to Bombay and other centres. Export of prawn from this District was of the order of Rs. 1.6 cores in 1982-83. There is however increased competition with relatively developed fishery in South Kanara District, in that, fish are mostly transported by lorries to Mangalore taking advantage of the construction of the West coast Highway running through the port towns of this District connecting Bombay with Cochin via Panaji and Mangalore.

Physical resource base analysed in the foregoing pages serves to bring out the diversified nature of the resources and potentials for their development. There are evidence of the exploitation of these resources mainly for export or utilisation elsewhere. For instance, the utilisation of water resources has been mainly for the production of hydro-electricity which is fed into the grid at Hubli for supply to main centres/areas of demand elsewhere in the State and for supply to neighbouring States. The District consumes very little of it; and it is mainly for domestic purposes often linked with irrigation of plantation crops by installing pumpsets. Because of the rugged terrain and sparse distribution of cultivated area and the population, harnessing the river waters by the construction of major reservoirs has not been of use to the benefit of the inhabitants of the area or for upgrading the land quality and land use. Similar instance is that of the major industry - West Coast Paper Mills - located at Dandeli (Haliyal Taluka) in the Northern-Malnad tract which having utilised bamboo and other wood products depends on these raw materials from area, as far as Madhya Pradesh. These are some of the essential considerations in formulating an integrated development strategy for the District.

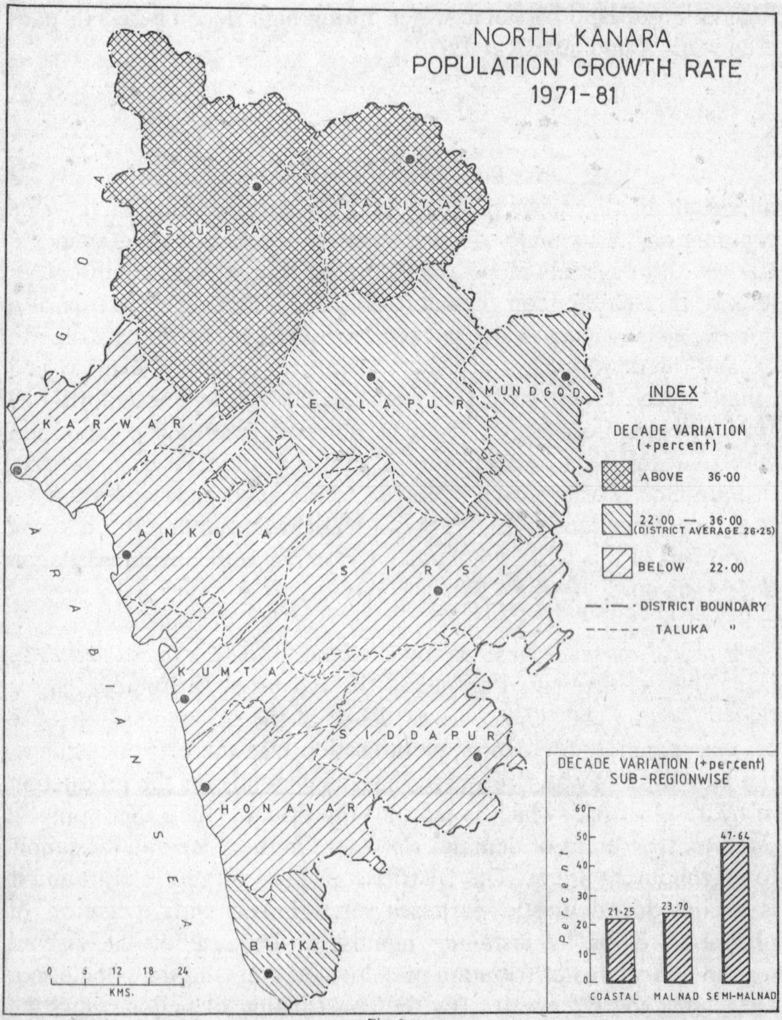

Fig. 9

5. Population

5.1 Pattern of Growth (Table 4)

Due to unsettled administrative and political conditions, frequent strife among the rulers, un favourable topographical and climatic conditions resulting in high incidence of mortality due to malaria and other diseases, the profile of population is one of low density, and low growth rate. From a base of 454,490 persons in 1901 the total population of the District in 1981 increased to 1,071,034 persons (+ 136 percent as against +165 percent in its coastal counter part of South Kanara District and +184 percent in the State as a whole). The pattern of increase in rural population during the same period is still lower i.e. +95 percent in North Kanara District as against +112 percent in South Kanara and + 131 percent in the State.

Table 4: North Kanara District - Pattern of Growth of Population (1901-81) - decadal variations

Year	Increase/Decrease	Population
1901	--	454,490
1911	-5.27	430,548
1921	-6.69	401,727
1931	+4.01	417,835
1941	+5.58	441,157
1951	+17.37	517,780
1961	+33.17	689,549
1971	+23.14	849,105
1981	+26.25	1,072,034

Source: *Census of India*, 1981, Series -9, Part II-A, Karnataka

Due to reasons mentioned above, inter-temporal variations show that until 1921 there was continuous decline in population. With increased accessibility, opening up of the area and declining incidence of disease and mortality, growth-rate started showing positive trend (+ 4.01 percent) during 1921-31[1]. The growth rate of +26.25 percent for the decade 1971-81 was almost the same as that of the State (+26.75 percent). Variations in the growth-ratc among Coastal, the Malnad and the Semi-Malnad sub-regions show that the Coastal and the Malnad tracts do not differ much (+21.63 percent and +23.7 percent respectively) while the Semi-Malnad recorded the highest growth-rate on account of inmigration following the construction of hydro-electric project and setting up of new industries around Dandeli. Within these sub-regions there are however significant variations, as for instance, in Bhatkal Taluka (in the coastal tract) which has predominantly Muslim population and has increasing trade with Bombay and Gulf countries. Here, the growth rate during 1971-81 was +35.22 percent (Table 5). In the Malnad tract too the area around Supa and Yellapur show a higher growth-rate (+46.00 percent and + 34.94 percent respectively).

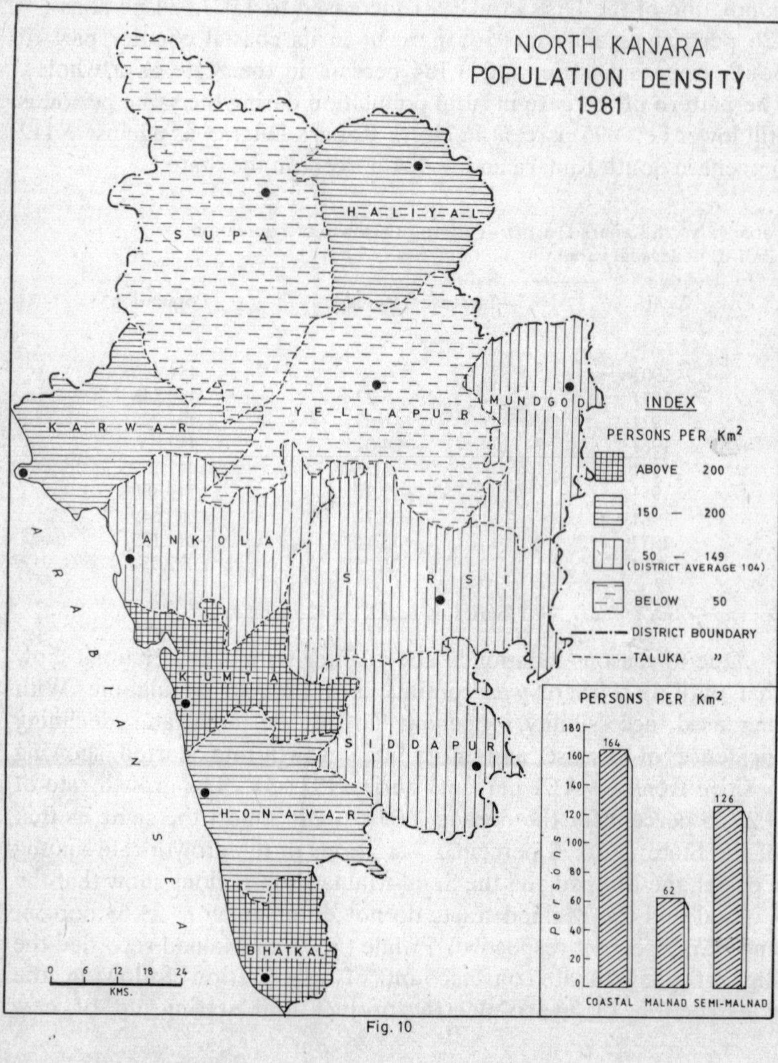

Fig. 10

Table 5 : North Kanara District - Population Density and Growth Rate (1971-81)

Sub-regions and talukas	Area Km^2	Population 1981	Population 1971	Density Persons Km^2 1981	Density Persons Km^2 1971	Growth rate percentage 1971-81
COASTAL	3336.5	548,901 51.0)*	451,284 (53.0)*	164	135	+21.25
Karwar	732.1	125,635	104,477	172	143	+20.63
Ankola	918.7	81,057	67,871	88	74	+19.43
Kumta	582.0	117,325	100,743	202	170	+16.46
Honavar	754.8	127,988	106,537	170	143	+20.13
Bhatkal	348.9	96,896	71,656	278	205	+35.22
MALNAD	5370.8	331,836 (31.0)*	268,250 (32.0)*	62	50	+23.70
Supa	1890.3	52,215	35,762	28	19	+46.00
Yellapur	1301.1	59,989	44,456	46	34	+34.94
Sirsi	1320.1	135,107	114,230	102	86	+18.28
Siddapur	859.3	84,525	73,802	98	86	+14.53
SEMI-MALNAD	1515.5	191,297 (18.0)8*	129,571 (15.0)*	126	85	+47.64
Haliyal	847.4	132,552	85,107	156	101	+55.74
Mundgod	668.1	58,745	44,464	88	67	+32.12
North Kanara District	10222.80	1072,034	849,105	104	83	+26.25
South Kanara District				282	230	+22.55
Karnataka				194	153	+226.75

* Figures in bracket denote percentage of population to the total population in the District.

5.2 **Population density - Spatial Variations** (Table 5)

Population density of the District is the lowest in the State; 104 persons per km^2 in contrast to the State average of 194 persons km^2. On the contrary its counter part - the South Kanara District stands third in the State with density as high as 282 persons per square km^2.

Intra-District variations in population bring out distinct characteristics of the Coastal, the Malnad and the Semi-Malnad tracts, in that the coastal area has the highest density of 164 persons km^2 followed by the Semi-Malnad having 126 persons km^2; the Malnad having the lowest density (62 persons km^2). Within the coastal tract it is the width of the alluvial plain and the extent of the latentic hills and uplands that account for variations. For example, the density varies from 88 persons km^2 in Ankola Taluka to 278 persons km^2 in Bhatkal taluka. Likewise, in the Malnad the hilly areas of Supa Taluka have the lowest density (28 persons km^2) and the highest is around Sirsi (102 persons km^2). In the Semi-Malnad too the variations as between Mundgod taluka and Haliyal taluka are sharp; 88 persons km^2 in Mundgod taluka as against 156 persons km^2 in Haliya taluka.

5.3 **Migration**:

What do these intra-district variations in population density and growth convey in terms of the spatial interactions or interrelationship among aspects of environment, physical resources and human response? Sex ratios provide some reflections into the possible out migration, male or female specific, depending on the characteristics of the Coastal, the Malnad and the Semi-Malnad (Table 6). Sex ratio for the District is generally on the lower side (958 females per 1000 males) which supports the trend towards marriage migration of females. Reason is obvious because the District has generally high level of literacy (57.35 percent in the case of male and 38.95 percent in the case of female and total literacy 48.35 percent) and most of the migrant families from the District who have permanently settled in Bombay prior to 1956 or later in and around Banglore prefer to have marriage alliance with the girls from the District[3]. So much is the affinity with the "home-District" that both in Bombay and Banglore there are Housing Colonies named after the migrants from North Kanara or South Kanara District. Within the District too the people are outward looking on account of limited opportunities for gainful employment under conditions of high level of literacy and professional skills that the younger population has acquired.

Further analysis of variations in sex ratio also reveals the fact that between the coastal and the Malnad tract it is the former which has the highest sex-ratio of 1003 females per 1000 males. On account of population pressure on the agricultural land coupled with high literacy there is outmigration of male population to cities outside the District. Till recently, it was the acute housing problems of the metropolitan centres such as Bombay and Banglore which dissuaded the migrants to leave female members of the family in the place of birth.

Table 6 : North Kanara District - Sex ratio (1981) (Females per 1000 Males)

Taluka	Sub-region	Sex ratio	Remark
	COASTAL	1003	**Male migration**
Karwar	"	999	
Ankola	"	974	
Kumta	"	992	
Honavar	"	1010	
Bhatkal	"	1037	
	MALNAD	**916**	**High female mortality and marriage migration**
Supa	"	885	
Yellapur	"	916	
Sirsi	"	916	
Siddapur	"	938	
	SEMI-MALNAD	**907**	High female mortality and marriage migration
Haliyal	"	916	
Mundgod	"	889	
North Kanara District		958	
South Kanara District		1059	
Karnataka State		962	

The organic link between the coastal plains, the foot hills and the Malnad are better revealed through seasonal migration[4]. For example, the coastal population depends on the foot hill interior for the supply of fodder for cattle and fuel wood. Trans-humance is another characteristic in which the livestock of the coastal plains is moved into the foot hill area of grass and grazing lands during the lean period of agricultural operation after transplantation of paddy in July until November.

Similarly the agricultural labourers of the coastal plains migrate to the Malnad area to work in plantation gardens which require perennial labour[5].

5.4 **Pattern of literacy** (Table 7)

The Coastal and the Malnad sub-regions is general have high level of literacy contrary to the general observation that areas which are relatively underdeveloped have low level of literacy[6]. Historical factors and the cultural and economic contacts which the District enjoyed being a part of the erstwhile Bombay Province have contributed to high level of literacy. The average literacy for the District in 1981 was 48.35 percent while the State average was 38.46 percent. In fact, the District occupies fourth position in respect of literacy in the State. The first ranking District is again the adjoining coastal District of South Kanara (53.46 percent). High level of literacy is observed in respect of male and female literacy too (57.35 percent and 38.95 percent respectively in contrast to male literacy of 48.81 percent and female literacy of 27.71 percent for the State).

Interesting feature is the spatial pattern of literacy. While the total literacy does not show wide variations among the Coastal, Malnad and the Semi-Malnad sub-regions female literacy is generally low in the Semi-Malnad. Accessibility to the town/trading centre, improved economic condition of spice-garden owners brings out variations in literacy rate within the Malnad; in that the areas around Sirsi and Siddapur have high literacy rate (total, male and female) while Supa and Yellapur in the northern part of Malnad have lower level of literacy - 23.25 percent). Variations in literacy among certain religions and communities are also revealing. Bhatkal taluka in the coastal tract has low level of literacy because of the higher percentage of Muslim population. Likewise, Ankola taluka in the coastal tract has *Nadar* community which is generally backward in comparison with the rest. This observation is true of parts of Semi-Malnad tract around Mundagod. Literacy rate is increasing as shown by the 1971 and 1981 data. Even in 1971, the District had a higher literacy rate than that of the State as a whole and maintained its fourth rank among the 19 Districts of the State in respect of literacy in 1971 and 1981.

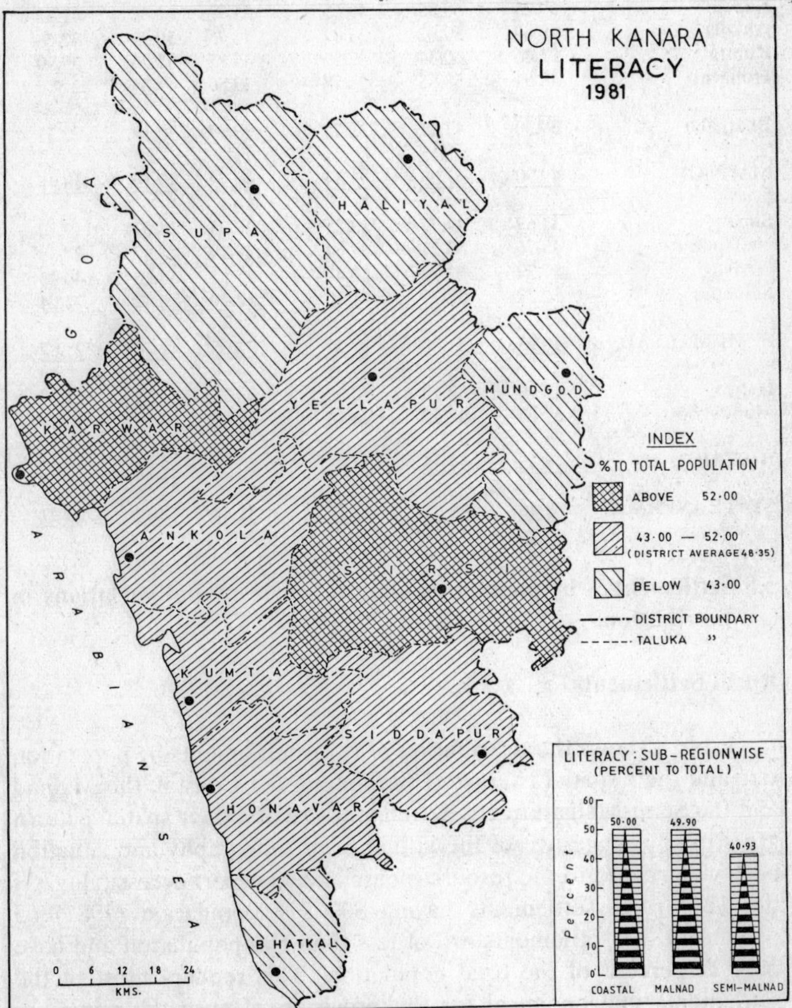

Fig. 11

Table 7 : North Kanara District - Pattern of Literacy (Percent to total population - 1971 and 1981)

Sub-region and Taluka	1981 Total	1981 Male	1981 Female	1971 Total	1971 Male	1971 Female
COASTAL	50.00	59.41	40.62	42.26	52.02	32.76
Karwar	59.25	68.95	49.55	51.73	62.36	41.52
Ankola	48.67	59.02	38.04	40.75	50.93	30.28
Kumta	51.46	60.34	42.51	45.85	55.86	35.90
Honavar	48.51	58.55	38.58	39.50	49.35	29.92
Bhatkal	39.30	47.11	31.76	28.97	36.18	22.31
MALNAD	49.90	57.55	41.54	41.79	49.10	13.45
Supa	34.67	44.77	23.25	26.95	34.07	19.10
Yellapur	45.76	53.21	37.64	37.29	45.87	27.48
Sirsi	57.37	63.74	50.42	47.92	54.10	40.75
Siddapur	50.27	58.79	41.10	42.20	50.42	32.94
SEMI-MALNAD	40.93	51.40	29.39	32.65	42.70	21.87
Haliyal	42.39	53.13	30.68	33.78	44.62	21.87
Mundagod	37.63	47.57	26.44	30.48	39.10	20.61
DISTRICT	48.35	57.35	38.95	40.65	49.59	31.30
STATE AVERAGE	38.46	48.81	27.71	31.52	41.62	20.97

5.5 Settlements - by population size and their spatial variations in distribution.

Rural Settlements

Table 8 shows the distribution of rural settlements by population size and their spatial characteristics among the Coastal, the Malnad and the Semi-Malnad tracts. Settlement size and their spatial pattern are strongly suggestive of the influence of topography and situation both with regard to the resources base and transport accessibility. Of the 1283 rural settlements having 800 241 population (1981) 65 percent of the settlements are of less than 500 population and have only 22 percent of the total population. This renders most of the settlements uneconomical for the provision of even the minimum level of infrastructure facilities and amenities not to speak of any small-scale industry based on local resources. In fact, nearly 86 percent of the settlements are of less than 1000 persons and they have approximately 44 percent of the rural population. At the other extreme only 84 settlements of over 2000 population constituting 6.55 percent of the total number of settlements have 37 percent of the total population. Of these there are 9 settlements of 5000-10000 population and 2 settlements are of over 10,000 population which do not qualify to have the status of a town; and they together have 10 percent of the total rural population. In the middle range of 500-2000 persons, there are 362 settlements (28.21 percent of the total) having nearly 41 percent of the total population. Spatial variations in the distribution of settlements and population by size ranges are more revealing than the overall pattern observed above. The coastal tract of high population density has 56 percent of its total population living in 64 large settlements (over 2000 persons) and these constitute only 15.65 percent of the total. These large settlements are located mostly in a linear pattern along the coastal plain strengthened by their linkage with towns situated at intervals along the same linear belt. In fact, of the 84 large settlements (> 2000 persons) of the District 64 of them(76 percent) are in the coastal tract and they have 81 percent of the total population of the District living in the large settlements of this size. In contrast, in the Malnad nearly 44 percent of the rural population lives in settlements of less than 500 persons which constitute nearly 76 percent of the total number of settlements in the Malnad. There are only 8 settlements of over 2000 persons and these are mostly the historically famous cultural economic centres which are now stagnant (e.g. Banavasi).Interestingly, Supa, the taluka Headquarters in the northern part of the Malnad - is not a town and classed as a large village[7]. These large settlements have only 8.55 percent of the rural population of the Malnad. In Supa taluka 84 percent of the rural settlements are of less than 500 persons having 47 percent of the rural population of the taluka. The Malnad alone has 62 percent of the total number of small settlements (< 500 persons) in the District and nearly 65 percent of the rural population dwelling in small settlements of the district is concentrated in this tract.

The transitional character of the Semi Malnad is reflected in the distribution of population in different size-range of settlements. On account of the western part of Semi-Malnad having somewhat the Malnad characteristics nearly 64 percent of the rural settlements of the Semi-Malnad are small (< 500 persons) and they have 22 percent of the rural population of this tract.

TABLE 8: North Kanara District-Rural Population Distributionin Different size Range of Settlements (1981)

Sub-Regions	Size of settle-ments (Persons)	No.	% to total No. of settlements	Commulative %	Population	% to total Population	Cummu-lative %
COASTAL							
Total No. of	<200	113	27.63	--	10,569	2.48	-
Settlements : 409	200-499	84	20.54	48.17	27,652	6.50	8.98
Population : 425, 364	500-999	87	21.27	69.44	63,473	14.92	23.90
	1000-1999	61	14.91	84.35	84,207	19.80	43.70
	2000-4999	53	12.96	97.31	155,699	36.60	80.30
	5000-9999	9	2.20	99.51	60,278	14.17	94.47
	10000+	2	0.49	100.00	23,483	5.53	100.00
MALNAD							
Total No. of	<200	243	35.53	-	23,575	8.92	-
Settlements : 684	200-499	276	40.35	75.88	91,554	34.64	43.56
Population : 264,326	500-999	123	17.98	93.86	83,382	31.54	75.10
	1000-1999	34	4.97	98.83	43,269	16.35	91.45
	2000-4999	8	1.17	100.00	23,146	8.55	100.00
SEMI-MALNAD							
Total No. of	<200	69	36.32	-	6,013	5.48	-
Settlements : 190	200-499	52	27.37	63.69	18,185	16.55	22.03
Population : 109,951	500-999	38	20.00	83.69	26,607	24.21	46.24
	1000-1999	19	10.00	93.68	26,088	23.74	69.98
	2000-4999	12	6.32	100.00	33,058	30.02	100.00
DISTRICT							
Total No. of	<200	425	33.13	-	40,157	5.02	-
Settlements : 1283	200-499	412	32.11	65.24	137,393	17.17	22.19
	500-999	248	19.33	84.57	173,462	21.68	43.87
Total Rural	1000-1999	114	8.88	93.45	153,564	19.19	63.06
Population : 800,241	2000-4999	73	5.69	99.14	211,903	26.48	89.54
	5000-9999	9	0.70	99.84	60,279	7.53	97.07
	10000+	2	0.16	100.00	23,483	2.93	100.00

Table 9: North Kanara District _ Distribution of Population in different size range of settlements - 1981

Taluka	Total villages	Population Rural	< 200 No. of villages	< 200 Population	200 - 499 No. of villages	200 - 499 Population	500 - 999 No. of villages-	500 - 999 Population	1000 - 1999 No. of villages	1000 - 1999 Population	2000 - 4999 No. of villages	2000 - 4999 Population	500 No. villa
0	1	2	3	4	5	6	7	8	9	10	11	12	13
District*	1283	800241	425	40157	412	137393	248	173462	114	153564	73	211903	9
			(33.12)	(5.02)	(32.11)	(19.33)	(19.33)	(21.68)	(8.88)	(19.19)	(5.69)	(26.48)	(0.7
Karwar	55	78425	8	821	11	4105	13	10028	13	18080	7	23073	3
			(14.54)	(1.05)	(20.00)	(5.23)	(23.64)	(12.79)	(23.64)	(23.05)	(12.73)	(29.42)	(5.4
Ankola	84	68904	20	1643	22	7084	24	16742	11	15336	6	20997	1
			(23.81)	(2.38)	(26.19)	(10.28)	(28.57)	(24.30)	(13.10)	(22.26)	(7.14)	(30.47)	1.19
Kumta	112	93940	40	4200	22	7194	22	15902	16	22209	10	26606	1
			(35.71)	(4.47)	(19.64)	(7.66)	(19.64)	(16.93)	(14.28)	(23.64)	(8.93)	(28.32)	(0.8
Honavar	95	112864	19	1661	20	6138	19	14071	14	19424	21	54022	1
			(20.00)	(1.47)	(21.05)	(5.44)	(20.00)	(12.47)	(14.74)	(17.21)	(22.10)	(47.86)	(1.0
Bhatkal	63	71231	26	2244	9	3131	9	6730	7	9158	9	31001	3
			(41.27)	(3.15)	(14.28)	(4.39)	(14.28)	(9.45)	(11.11)	(12.86)	(14.28)	(43.52)	(4.7
Supa	137	47293	63	5710	52	16457	14	9048	5	7032	3	9046	-
			(45.98)	(12.07)	(37.96)	(34.80)	(10.22)	(19.13)	(3.65)	(14.87)	(2.19)	(19.13)	
Yellapur	127	48197	55	5316	43	13220	18	12381	8	9595	3	7685	-
			(43.31)	(11.03)	(33.86)	(27.43)	(14.17)	(25.69)	(6.30)	(19.91)	(2.36)	(15.94	
Sirsi	226	96200	58	6813	100	34300	59	39877	7	8795	2	6415	-
			(25.66)	(7.08)	(44.25)	(35.65)	(26.11)	(41.45)	(3.10)	(9.14)	(0.88)	(6.67)	
Siddapur	194	73236	67	5736	81	27577	32	22076	14	17847	-	-	-
			(34.54)	(7.83)	(41.75)	(37.65)	(16.49)	(30.14)	(7.22)	(24.37)			
Haliyal	111	61538	39	2976	34	11388	22	16014	10	14648	6	16512	-
			(35.13)	(4.84)	(30.63)	(18.51)	(19.82)	(26.02)	(9.01)	(23.80)	(5.40)	(26.83)	
Mundgod	79	48413	30	3037	18	6797	16	10593	9	11440	6	16546	-
			(37.97)	(6.27)	(22.78)	(14.04)	(20.25)	(21.88)	(11.39)	(23.63)	(7.59)	(34.18)	

District* 10000 +	Honavar 10000 +	Kumta 10000 +
2 23483	1 12398	1 11085
(0.16) (2.93)	(1.05) (10.99)	(0.89) (11.80)

* Figures in bracket are in percent to total number of settlements/population

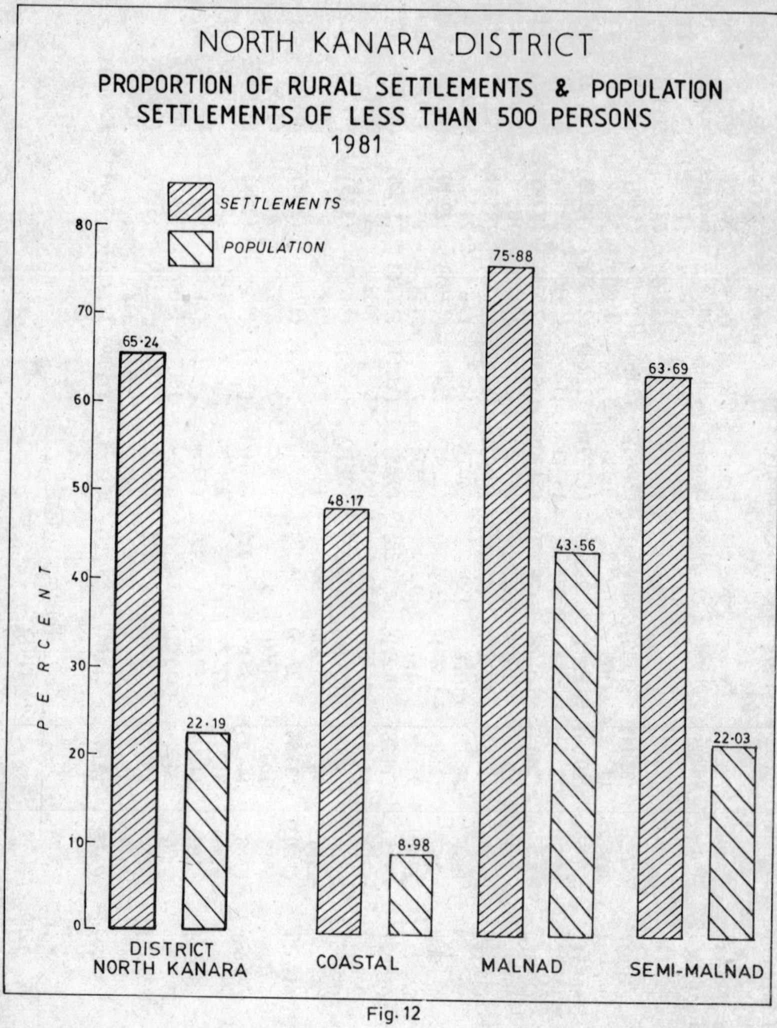

Fig. 12

Likewise, the percentage of large rural settlements (> 2000 population) also seems to be higher than that in the Malnad (6.32 per cent with 30 per cent of the rural population of Semi-Malnad).

Urban Settlements and pattern of Urbanization (Tables 10-12)

The number of towns in the District has increased from 8 in 1971 to 13 in 1981. There has been fluctuation in the number of towns since 1901 from 7 to 13 more because of the changes in the census definition of towns than by the emergence of new towns. Of the 8 towns in 1971, four (Karwar, Kumta, Honavar and Bhatkal) were in coastal area each being also the Headquarters of the talukas except Ankola which did not have the status of a town though being the taluka headquarters. All the four towns had the status of town since 1901. In the Malnad, there were only two towns - Sirsi and Yellapur. Sirsi being on the ancient trade route linking the port towns with the Deccan Plateau area was a town even n 1901 though it had only 6964 persons. Yellapur was not classed as town until 1971. This was because of inaccessibility and the dominant influence of Sirsi as a trading centre for the plantation crops of the Malnad as well as for trade with the coastal and the plateau area. With the construction of another road linking Karwar in the coastal area and Hubli in the plateau through Yellapur, this town has witnessed high growth rate (+ 88.00 per cent) during the decade 1971-81. The Semi-Malnad had two towns Haliyal the taluka headquarters and a rapidly growing industrial town--Dandeli which emerged as town in 1961 with the location of the West Coastal Paper Mills.

In 1981, three taluka headquarters attained the status of town anew - Ankola in the coastal area, Siddapur in the Malnad and Mundgod in the Simi-Malnad. In addition, two settlements - Ambikanagar (close to the industrial town of Dandeli in Semi-Malnad), and Ganeshgudi (In Malnad - near Supa), were designated as towns for the first time. These trends reflect the changing economic scene of the Malnad and the Semi-Malnad from a traditional agricultural economy depending on forest and plantation products to the emergence of processing industries based on local raw materials and related trading activity though on a small scale.

Pattern of urbanization measured by the proportion of urban population to the total and the urban structure however reveal sharp contrasts. While the percentage of urban population to the total for the District has increased from 17.73 percent in 1971 to 25.42 percent in 1981, Semi-Malnad shows the highest level of Urbanization (45.2 per cent) followed by 22.6 per cent in the Coastal area. The Malnad is still least urbanised with only 18.68 per cent of the population being urban.

Table 10 : North Kanara District - Pattern of Urbanization (Talukawise) - 1971

Taluka and Sub-region	Urban Population % to total	Total No.	Towns I	II	III	IV	V	VI
COASTAL	**17.26**							
Karwar	26.58	1	-	-	1	-	-	-
Ankola	00.00	-	-	-	-	-	-	-
Kumta	19.04	1	-	-	-	1	-	-
Honavar	11.45	1	-	-	-	1	-	-
Bhatkal	26.14	1	-	-	-	1	-	-
MALNAD	**14.93**							
Supa	00.00	-	-	-	-	-	-	-
Yellapur	14.12	1	-	-	-	-	1	-
Sirsi	25.01	1	-	-	1	-	-	-
Siddapur	00.00	-	-	-	-	-	-	-
SEMI-MALNAD	**40.86**							
Haliyal	44.17	2	-	-	1	1	-	-
Mundagod	00.00	-	-	-	-	-	-	-
District	17.73	8	-	-	3	4	1	-

ClassI: 100,000 + Population II: 100,000 - 50,000 Population
III: 50,000 - 20,000 Population IV: 20,000 - 10,000 Population
V: 10000 - 5,000 Population VI: < 5000 "

Table 11 : North Kanara District - Pattern of Urbanisation (Talukawise) - 1981

Taluka and Sub-region		Urban Population % to total	Total No.	I	II	III	IV	V	VI
	COASTAL	22.60	5	-	-	3	2	-	-
Karwar	"	37.58	1	-	-	1	-	-	-
Ankola	"	15.00	1	-	-	-	1	-	-
Kumta	"	19.33	1	-	-	1	-	-	-
Honavar	"	12.23	1	-	-	-	1	-	-
Bhatkal	"	26.49	1	-	-	1	-	-	-
	MALNAD	<u>18.68</u>	<u>4</u>	-	-	<u>1</u>	<u>2</u>	-	<u>1</u>
Supa	"	9.43	1	-	-	-	-	-	1
Yellapur	"	19.66	1	-	-	-	1	-	-
Sirsi	"	28.80	1	-	-	1	-	-	-
Siddapur	"	13.36	1	-	-	-	1	-	-
	SEMI-MALNAD	<u>45.20</u>	<u>4</u>	-	-	<u>1</u>	<u>2</u>	<u>1</u>	-
Haliyal	"	53.72	3	-	-	1	1	1	-
Mundgod	"	17.59	1	-	-	-	1	-	-
District		25.42	13	-	-	5	6	1	1

Table 12 : North Kanara District - Population size and Pattern of growth of towns (1901-81) - Decade Variations (%)

Sub-region and Town	1901	1911	1921	1931	1941	1951	1961	1971	1981	% to total popu-lation	% of urban Popu-tion in region
COASTAL									**124,076**	**22.60**	**45.53**
Karwar	9648	18,159	12,861	14,147	15,812	19,764	23,906	27,770	47,218		
		(+88.22)	(-29.18)	(+10.00)	(+11.77)	(+24.99)	(+20.96)	(+16.16)	(+70.00)		
Ankola	--	--	--	--	--	--	--	--	12,153		
Kumta	6711	6,609	10,650	10,919	12,466	14,890	16,223	19,112	23,385		
		(-1.52)	(+61.14)	(+2.53)	(+14.17)	(+19.44)	(+8.95)	(+17.81)	(+22.36)		
Honavar	6929	7,191	6,837	7,654	8,939	9,714	10,453	12,163	19,655		
		(+3.78)	(-4.92)	(+11.95)	(+16.69)	(+6.67)	(+7.61)	(+19.5)	(+21.54)		
Bhatkal	6,964	7141	6,982	8,686	10,718	12,167	15,070	18,732	25,665		
		(+2.54)	(-2.23)	(+24.41)	(+23.39)	(+13.52)	(+23.86)	(+24.30)	(+37.01)		
MALNAD	--	--	--	--	--	--	--	--	**66,910**	**20.16**	**24.55**
Ganeshgudi(Supa T)	--	--	--	--	--	--	--	--	4,922		
Yellapur	--							6,275	11,792		
									(+87.42)		
Sirsi	6,125	6,372	6,268	7,109	10,451	13,226	21,240	28,576	38,907		
		(+4.08)	(-1.63)	(+13.42)	(+47.01)	(+26.55)	(+60.59)	(+34.54)	(+36.15)		
Siddapur	--	--	--	--	--	--	--	--	11,289		
SEMI-MALNAD	--	--	--	--	--	--	--	--	**81.535**	**42.62**	**29.92**
Ambikanagar(Haliyal T)		--	--	--	--	--	--	--	7,923		
Haliyal	3,282	5,505	4,835	5,436	6,448	8,184	10,343	12,163	15,655		
		(+67.73)	(-12.17)	(+12.43)	(+18.62)	(+26.92)	(+26.38)	(+17.60)	(+28.71)		
Dandeli(Haliyal T)		--	--	--	--	--	7,989	25,425	47,625		
								(+218.25)	(+87.32)		
Mundgod	--	--	--	--	--	--	--	--	10.332		

Note : Figures in bracket are growth rates +/- percent.

FIG 13

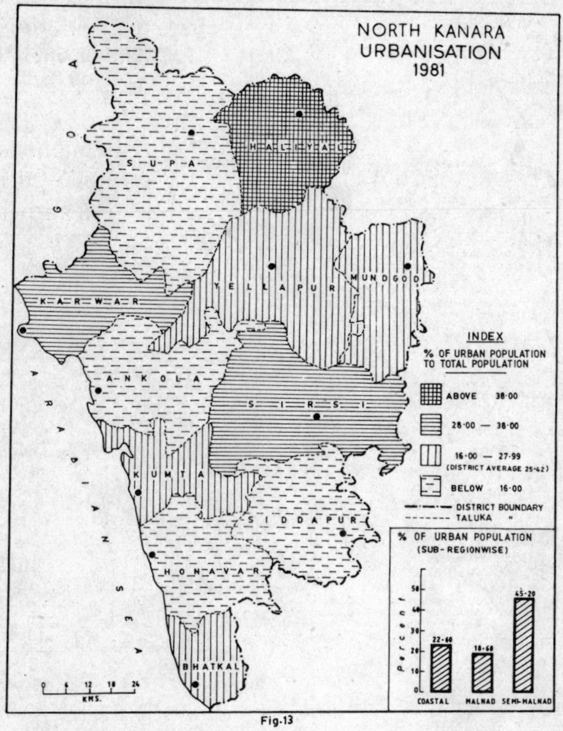

Fig-13

There is no class I or class II city in the District. The five class III towns (Karwar, Sirsi and Dandeli) have been growing very rapidly and are about to reach the class II city status. That industry and trade are catalysts for growth are illustrated by the growth rate of these towns during 1971-81. Karwar a port town and District headquarters though under the shadow of Panaji-Marmagoa in the north, is now growing taking advantage of the development of Karwar as an all weather port. Naval base is proposed to be developed in the coming years. Being at the mouth of the Kali River and with the exploitation of the river water for hydro-power development in the State, there is a need to develop the Kali Basin in an integrated manner.

Among the coastal towns all are port-towns and await development being located along the linear belt of high population density. Likewise, upgrading the taluka headquarters by infrastructure facilities and amenities would strengthen their status as trading centres

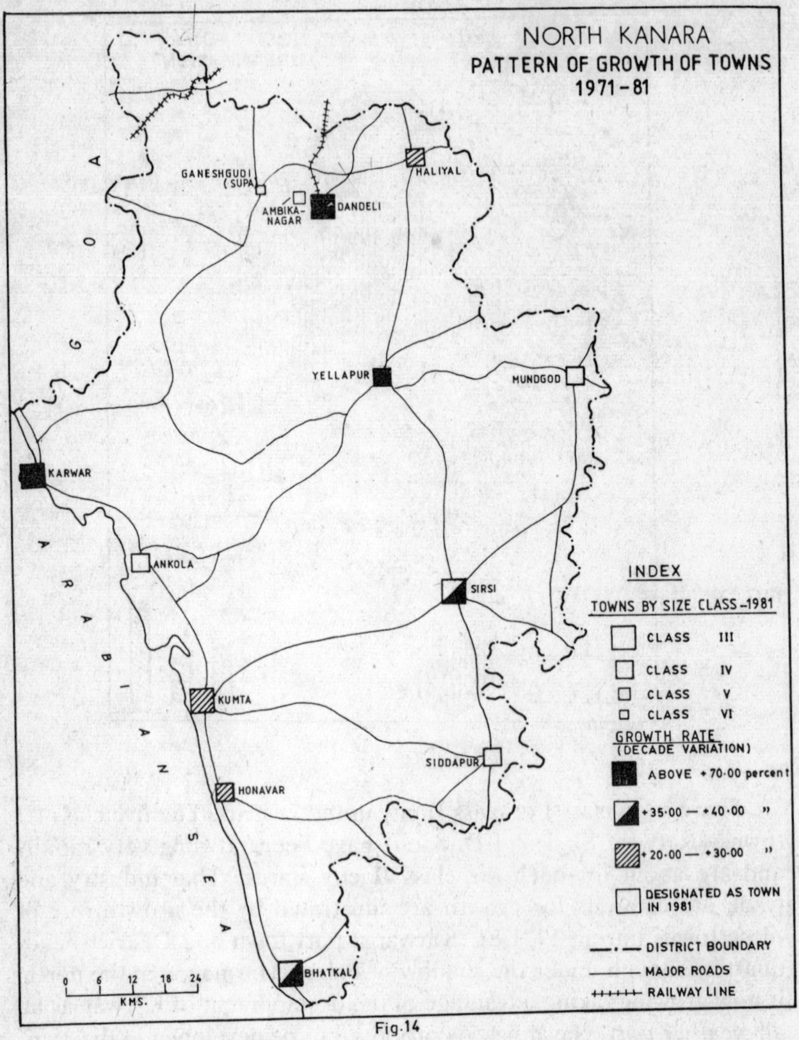

Fig.14

The foregoing study of the physical and the human resources show marked spatial affinity and contrasts which enable us to treat them separately in the first instance with a view to identify the gaps in their development. Thus, in the coastal area fishery awaits exploitation as an industry comparable to its development elsewhere in the West coast. Land use and cropping pattern in the coastal plains and the foot hill areas need to be assessed from the point of view of their complementarity. The Malnad sub-region even in its initial level of exploitation of its forest, mineral and plantation crops is showing signs of environmental degradation which poses a threat to its own development as well as of the interdependent economies of the coastal sub-region, the entire Malnad sub-region of the State and of the State as a whole. For the transitional semi-Malnad region, its transitional characteristics could be exploited to its advantage rather than its undergoing the stresses and strains of the urban pull of the plateau region and the peripheral situation with reference to the development in the core region of the Malnad.

Human resources reflect higher level of development in respect of literacy and intra-regional and inter-regional interactions. This could be an advantage to reverse the trend of development in which the skill of the people and the physical resources could be blended for rapid development as in other parts of the Malnad e.g. Shimoga, Hassan and Coorg. areas.

NOTES

1. This trend in growth rate is similar for the entire Malnad region of Karnataka.
2. Rugged topography, forests and low density of population are the characteristics of the Malnad.
3. Based on personal communication with the author.
4. Based on local enquiry.
5. Seasonal migration is common between the coastal and the Malnad regions.
6. Census of India, 1981 : Series 9, *Karnataka - Primary census Abstract* Part II B(i), Map, 3, p.5
7. Supa is now being vacated because of the submergence by the proposed Kali River Hydropower project.

FIVE

Spatial Organisation of Economic Activities - Infrastructure Facilities and Amenitiesz and Industries

The factors that contribute to the emergence of few but selected number of human settlements as nodes are situation, demographic and socio-economic attributes of settlements and the availability of infrastructure facilities and amenities. It has been observed in the foregoing analysis that the longitudinal extent of the coastal plains and the linear pattern of distribution of settlements have resulted in the concentration of population and growth of few villages and towns as nodal centres. Four out of five towns (including Karwar the District Headquarters) are port owns which have witnessed growth and decline in the historical past; and they show signs of revival under stresses and strains as a result of new pattern of functional-economic linkages that are superimposed on the old one. In the foothill interiors of the coastal region though transport routes have brought many small settlements within easy reach of towns in the coastal plains, it is the initial size of settlements and small extent of cultivated areas (of mainly plantation crops and paddy) that restricts their growth as nodal centres. In the Malnad and the Semi-Malnad tracts the historically famous centres like Banavasi (Sirsi Taluka) and Bilgi (Siddapur taluka) have declined and owing to the rapid growth of trading towns like Sirsi and Sagar (across the District border in Shimoga taluka) their revival has been further restricted. Moreover, centres like Mundgod and Haliyal on account of their proximity (50 kms. and 32 kms. respectively) to the twin city complex of Hubli-Darwar with much higher order infrastructure facilities and economic functions are increasingly drawn towards the latter for economic transactions.

Infrastructure facilities

1. **Roads** : Among these, two roads are the vital links among settlements within the District, while the metre gauge railway line touches only the northern fringe of the District connecting Dandeli the industrial town in Haliyal taluka with Alnavar on the Miraj-Bangalore Section of the railway line in Karnataka.[1] The maritime occean routes also await revival in the context of the development of numerous ports along the West Coast.

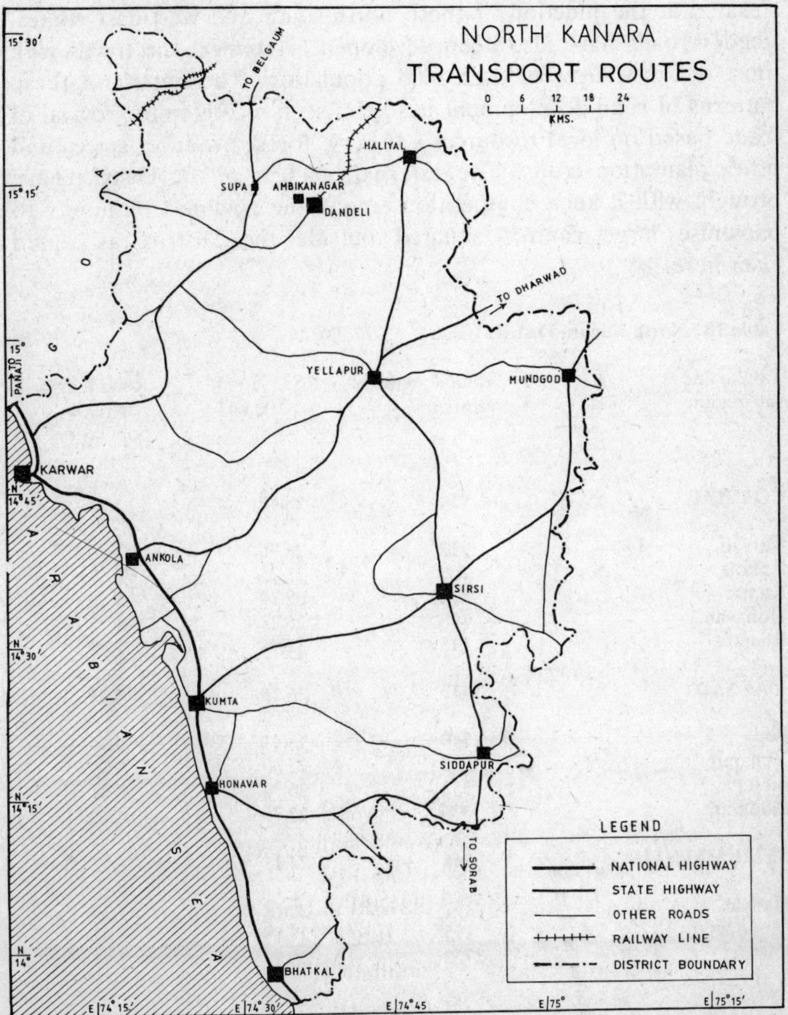

Fig. 15

The analysis of road network reveals that the basic spatial pattern of linkages strengthening the process of emergence of nodal settlements has been well laid out either by improving the old routes or construction of the new ones (Fig.15). The important links that have emerged anew are the two north-south routes, West Coast Highway (National Highway) connecting Bombay with Cochin through all the towns in the coast and the State highway running through the Malnad. The transverse routes connecting the coastal and the Malnad sub-regions have also been strengthened. This has strengthened the development of the Malnad towns as they are situated at the junction of these north-south and west-east routes. Feeder roads have also been developed to connect the towns with most of the villages of over 1000 population. The impact of these patterns of road development has been seen mostly in the revival of trade based on local resources - fishery, forest produce, spices and other plantation crops. The external linkages of the District have brought with it keen competition among the trading community to patronise large centres situated outside the District as stated elsewhere.

Table 13 : North Kanara District - Roads (1977-78)

Taluka and sub-region	Road length (Kms.)	Road length per 100 km^2	Road length per 1,000 population
COASTAL	**956**	**28.65**	**1.74**
Karwar	212	28.96	1.69
Ankola	209	22.75	2.58
Kumta	222	38.14	1.89
Honavar	198	26.23	1.55
Bhatkal	115	32.96	1.19
MALNAD	**1410**	**26.25**	**4.25**
Supa	348	18.41	6.66
Yellapur	333	25.60	5.55
Sirsi	353	26.74	2.61
Siddapur	376	43.76	4.45
SEMI-MALNAD	**366**	**24.15**	**1.91**
Haliyal	171	20.18	1.29
Mundagod	195	29.19	3.32
District	2732	26.55	2.55

On an average road length per 100 km^2 area is 26.55 kms. for the District as against 28.65 kms in the Semi-Malnad (Table 13). In terms of the population served the Malnad seems to be better served (4.25 kms road length per 1000 population) though in reality it is the reverse. This is on account of the fact that the Malnad is an area of low density of population and the settlements are small and scattered. In contrast, in the coastal area road length per 1000 population is only 1.76 kms. Yet, the linear pattern of population distribution along the West Coast Highway has brought a larger percentage of population within easy reach of towns and large villages. The Semi-Malnad also shows a pattern similar to that of the coastal region but it is the higher level of population density and not the spatial pattern that brings out the similarity between the two sub-regions.

2. **Electricity** (Table 14)

The District ranks high both in terms of endogenously available hydro-power resources - existing production and potential and also in terms of access to electricity. Even in 1977-78, 41 percent of all the villages and towns had access to electricity. Its use has been mostly for domestic lighting though recent trend has been to energise pumpsets for irrigating the garden lands both in the coastal and the Malnad sub-regions. On account of the variations in population size and spatial arrangement, 53 percent of the human settlements in the coastal tract had access to electricity as against 33.6 percent in the Malnad and 42.78 percent in the Semi-Malnad.

In the coastal tract households being in the midst of co-conut gardens it is the well water that is used for irrigation as well as for domestic purposes by the use of electricity. In the Malnad area perennial water supply by tributary streams to the spice gardens did not necessitate, till recently, the use of pumpset for irrigation. However, degradation of forest resources and subsequent erosion have been responsible for incision of the perennial valleys perforcing the farmers to use pumpset for lifting water from the river bed. The Kali River Project which is well under way, would ensure supply of electricity not only to the District but for other parts of the State as well. However, available data and local enquiry reveals a disquieting feature, in that, the exploitation of water and power resources has been largely to meet the demand outside the District.

Table 14 : North Kanara District - Extent of Electrification (1977-78)

Taluka and Sub-region	Total No. and villages and towns	No. of towns villages electrified	% to total	No. of Pump-sets	Average cultivated area per pump-set (hectares)
COASTAL	**414**	**220**	**53.14**	**2582**	**18.12**
Karwar	56	24	42.86	1000	105.00
Ankola	85	46	54.12	441	20.52
Kumta	113	60	53.10	637	16.46
Honavar	96	64	66.67	1068	9.59
Bhatkal	64	26	40.63	336	19.33
MALNAD	**690**	**232**	**33.62**	**729**	**56.66**
Supa	138	13	9.42	11	595.82
Yellapur	128	29	22.66	71	111.21
Sirsi	227	122	53.74	539	29.13
Siddapur	197	68	34.52	108	103.31
SEMI-MALNAD	**194**	**83**	**42.78**	**106**	**292.46**
Haliyal	114	50	43.86	80	236.29
Mundgod	80	33	41.25	26	465.31
District	1298	535	41.22	3417	34.85

Source : Uttar Kannada District 1977-78, *An Economic Review.*

3. **Other facilities and amenities** (Tables 15-18)

The District has a higher literacy rate (48.35 percent total, 57.35 percent male and 38.95 percent female) and the available facilities for education - particularly the primary education reveals that the coastal tract is better off wherein one primary school serves on an average an area of 4 km^2 while for the Malnad and the Semi-Malnad the corresponding values are 8.76 km^2 and 8.86km^2 respectively. This reflects on the population size of settlements and the spatial pattern of distribution and is borne out by the number of settlements served by one primary school. In the case of higher secondary school the area served again shows variations characteristic of the region's topography, accessibility and size of settlements. All the towns have atleast one College although larger centres like Karwar, Sirsi and Kumta have diversified higher educational facility comprising Arts and Science, Law and Commerce. The agricultural prosperity of the Malnad and the limited employment avenues for the relatively poor

Table-15 :North Kanara District - Educational facilities -(1977-78)

		Educational In Institution								
Taluka	Sub-region	No. of primary schools (P. S.)	Area served (average) km^2	No. of settle-ments served by one P.S	No. of High schools (H.S.) km^2	Area served by onef (H. S.)	No. of settle-ments served	No. of colleges & Tech. Institu-tions	Area served by one college & Tech. Insttn.	No. of settlement served by one Insti-tute
	COASTAL	**803**	**4.15**	**0.52**	**78**	**42.77**	**5.31**	**12**	**278.04**	**34.5**
Karwar		209	3.50	0.27	30	24.40	1.87	6	122.02	9.33
Ankola		124	7.41	0.68	9	102.10	9.44	1	918.7	85.00
Kumta		170	3.42	0.66	15	38.80	7.53	3	194.0	37.66
Honavar		197	3.83	0.49	17	44.40	5.65	1	754.8	96.00
Bhatkal		103	3.39	0.62	7	49.84	9.14	1	348.9	64.00
	MALNAD	**613**	**8.76**	**1.13**	**37**	**145.15**	**18.65**	**4**	**1342.7**	**172.5**
Supa		118	16.10	1.17	3	630.1	46.00	-	-	-
Yellapur		118	11.03	1.08	4	325.31	32.00	-	-	-
Sirsi		217	6.08	1.05	18	73.34	12.61	3	440.03	75.66
Siddapur		160	5.37	1.23	12	71.61	16.42	1	859.3	197.00
	SEMI-MALNAD	**171**	**8.86**	**1.13**	**10**	**151.55**	**19.40**	**1**	**1515.5**	**194.00**
Haliyal		97	8.74	1.17	8	105.92	14.25	1	847.4	114.00
Mundgod		74	9.03	1.08	2	334.05	40.00	-	-	-
District		1587	6.48	0.82	125	82.33	10.38	17	605.35	76.35

Table 16 : North District - Banking facilities (1977-78)

Taluka and Sub-region	Banks Comme-rcial	Co-op-erative	Total	Area served by one Bank km^2	No. of settle-ments served by one	Popula-ation served by one Bank
COASTAL	**59**	**12**	**71**	**46.99**	**5.83**	**7,731**
Karwar	19	3	22	33.28	2.55	5,711
Ankola	6	2	8	114.84	10.62	10,132
Kumta	15	2	17	34.24	6.65	6,901
Honavar	11	3	14	53.91	6.86	9,142
Bhatkal	8	2	10	34.89	5.40	8,453
MALNAD	**26**	**15**	**41**	**131.00**	**16.83**	**8,094**
Supa	5	4	9	210.03	15.33	5,802
Yellapur	5	3	8	162.64	16.00	7,499
Sirsi	11	4	15	88.01	15.13	9,007
Siddapur	5	4	9	95.48	21.89	9,392
SEMI-MALNAD	**16**	**4**	**20**	**75.77**	**9.7**	**9,565**
Haliyal	12	2	14	60.53	8.14	9,468
Mundgod	4	2	6	111.35	13.33	9,791
District	101	31	132	77.96	9.83	8,121

Table 17 : North Kanara District - Postal facilities 1977-78

Taluka and sub-region	Post Offices Post and telegraph	Post Office	Total	No. of settle-ments served by one Post-Office
COASTAL	**60**	**151**	**211**	**1.96**
Karwar	11	36	47	1.19
Ankola	10	18	28	3.04
Kumta	25	33	58	1.95
Honavar	8	47	55	1.75
Bhatkal	6	17	23	2.78
MALNAD	**30**	**138**	**168**	**4.11**
Supa	4	18	22	6.27
Yellapur	8	25	33	3.88
Sirsi	17	46	63	3.60
Siddapur	1	49	50	3.94
SEMI-MALNAD	**9**	**52**	**61**	**3.18**
Haliyal	7	35	42	2.71
Mundagod	2	17	19	4.21
District	99	341	440	2.95

Table 18 : North Kanara District - Health facilities 1977-78

Taluka and sub-region	Health Units: Hospitals	Dispensaries	Primary Health centres	Total	Area served by one H.Unit Km^2	No. of settlements served by H.U	Population per Health Unit
COASTAL	**2**	**17**	**5**	**24**	**139.02**	**17.25**	**22,871**
Karwar	1	3	1	5	146.42	11.20	25,127
Ankola	-	2	1	3	306.23	28.33	27,019
Kumta	-	5	1	6	97.00	18.83	19,554
Honavar	-	6	1	7	107.83	13.71	18,284
Bhatkal	1	1	1	3	116.30	21.33	32,299
MALNAD	**1**	**19**	**4**	**24**	**223.78**	**28.75**	**13,826**
Supa	-	4	1	5	378.06	27.60	10,443
Yellapur	-	7	1	8	162.64	16.00	07,499
Sirsi	1	3	1	5	264.02	45.40	27,021
Siddapur	-	5	1	6	143.22	32.83	14,087
SEMI-MALNAD	**2**	**5**	**2**	**9**	**168.39**	**21.55**	**21,255**
Haliyal	2	3	1	6	141.23	19.00	22,092
Mundgod	-	2	1	3	222.70	26.67	19,581

people (otherwise having higher level of literacy) have induced out-migration of younger people for specialised education and ultimately for settling outside the District.

In terms of Banking facilities one Bank serves an area of 46.99 km^2 in the coastal tract, 131 km^2 area in the Malnad and 75.77 km^2 in the Semi-Malnad. On an average there is one Bank for about 6 settlements in the coastal tract, 17 settlements in the Malnad and 10 settlements in the Semi-Malnad. Population served by one Bank is around 8000 persons for the District with slight variation among the three sub-regions.

Postal facilities again show marked variations with increased concentration in the coastal tract (1 Post Office serving approximately 2 settlements in the coastal tract in contrast to 4 in the Malnad and 3 in the Semi-Malnad.

Health facilities are inadequate considering the fact that there are only 5 hospitals - two each in the coastal and the Semi-Malnad tract while there is only 1 hospital in the Malnad. Seven out of 11 taluka headquarters do not have a hospital. The dispensaries and primary health centres do not provide any specialised treatment. In terms of the area covered and the number of settlements served also, all the three types of health facilities taken together reflect the inadequacy. This is corroborated by local enquiry which reveals that for any specialised treatment the people are required to visit Mangalore or Hubli at distances varying from 50 kms to 250 kms.

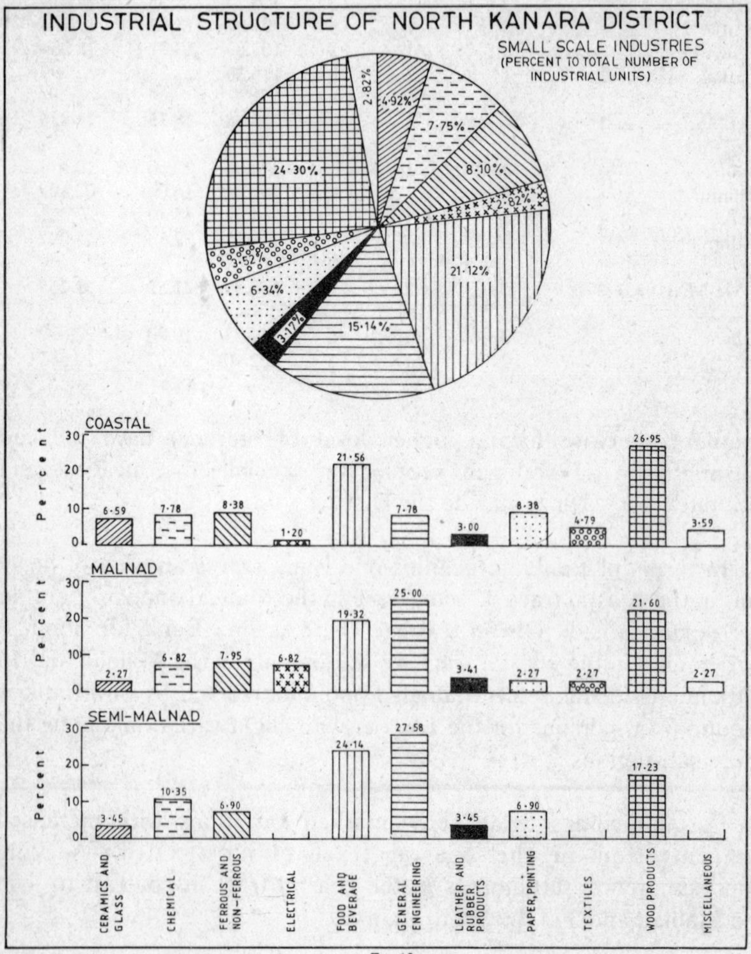

Fig.16

4. **Industries** (Tables 19-22)

The District is one of the least industrialised area. But for two medium sized factory industries - the West Coast Paper Mills at Dandeli in the Malnad and the Caustic Soda Factory at Binga near Karwar in the coastal tract, all other industries are of small scale using local raw materials.

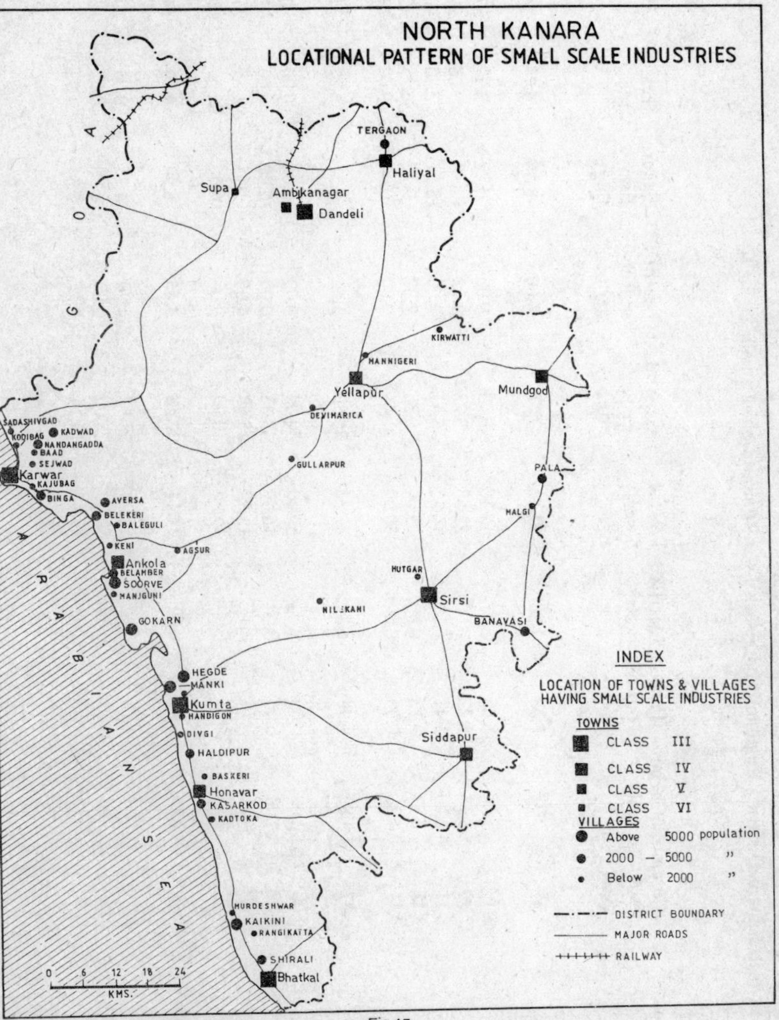

Fig.17

Table 19 : North Kanara District - Regional Characteristics in composition of small scale industry

Sub-region and Taluka	Ceramics & glass	Chemicals	Ferrous & Ferrous	Electricals	Industries Food & beverage	General Engineering	Leather Rubber products	Paper Printing	Textile	Wood products	Misc.	Total
COASTAL	**6.59**	**7.78**	**8.38**	**1.20**	**21.56**	**7.78**	**3.00**	**8.38**	**4.79**	**26.95**	**3.59**	**100.00**
Karwar	3.77	15.10	18.88	3.77	15.10	9.43	0.00	3.77	3.77	22.64	3.77	100.00
Ankola	12.90	3.23	3.23	0.00	22.58	3.23	3.23	12.90	9.68	29.02	0.00	100.00
Kumta	8.11	2.70	5.41	0.00	16.22	5.41	2.70	13.51	2.70	40.54	2.70	100.00
Honavar	3.13	3.13	3.13	0.00	25.00	6.25	9.37	9.37	6.25	25.00	9.37	100.00
Bhatkal	7.14	14.28	0.00	0.00	50.00	21.44	0.00	0.00	0.00	7.14	0.00	100.00
MALNAD	**2.27**	**6.82**	**7.95**	**6.82**	**19.32**	**25.00**	**3.41**	**2.27**	**2.27**	**21.60**	**2.27**	**100.00**
Supa	0.00	0.00	0.00	0.00	50.00	50.00	0.00	0.00	0.00	0.00	0.00	100.00
Yellapur	16.67	0.00	0.00	0.00	16.67	33.33	0.00	0.00	0.00	33.33	0.00	100.00
Sirsi	1.35	8.11	6.76	8.11	18.92	25.68	4.05	1.35	1.35	21.52	2.70	100.00
Siddapur	0.00	0.00	33.36	0.00	16.66	0.00	0.00	16.66	16.66	0./00	100.00	
SEMI-MALNAD	**3.45**	**10.35**	**6.90**	**0.00**	**24.14**	**27.58**	**3.45**	**6.90**	**0.00**	**17.23**	**0.00**	**100.00**
Haliyal	4.76	14.29	9.52	0.00	14.29	28.57	4.70	4.76	0.00	19.05	0.00	100.00
Mundagod	0.00	0.00	0.00	0.00	50.00	25.00	0.00	12.50	0.00	12.50	0.00	100.00
District	4.92	7.75	8.10	2.82	21.12	15.14	3.17	6.34	3.52	24.30	2.82	100.00

Table 20 : North Kanara District - Pattern of concentration of small scale industries

Sub-region and Taluka	Industries										
	Ceramics & glass	Chemi-cals	Ferrous & non-Ferrous	Electr-icals	Food and beverage	General Enginee-ring	Leather Rubbber products	Paper Print-ing	Textile	Wood pro-ducts	Misc.
COASTAL	**78.57**	**59.10**	**60.87**	**25.00**	**60.00**	**30.23**	**55.55**	**77.78**	**80.00**	**65.22**	**75.00**
Karwar	14.26	36.36	43.47	25.00	13.33	11.62	00.00	11.11	20.00	17.39	25.00
Ankola	28.58	4.55	4.35	0.00	11.67	2.33	11.11	22.22	30.00	13.04	00.00
Kumta	21.43	4.55	8.70	00.00	10.00	4.65	11.11	27.78	10.00	21.74	12.50
Honavar	7.15	4.55	4.35	00.00	13.33	4.65	33.33	16.67	20.00	11.60	37.50
Bhatkal	7.15	9.09	00.00	00.00	11.67	6.98	00.00	00.00	00.00	1.45	00.00
MALNAD	**14.29**	**27.27**	**30.43**	**75.00**	**28.34**	**51.16**	**33.33**	**11.11**	**20.00**	**27.54**	**25.00**
Supa	00.00	00.00	00.00	00.00	1.67	2.33	00.00	00.00	00.00	00.00	00.00
Yellapur	7.14	00.00	00.00	00.00	1.67	4.65	00.00	00.00	00.00	2.90	00.00
Sirsi	7.14	27.27	21.73	75.00	23.34	44.19	33.33	5.56	10.00	23.19	25.00
Siddapur	00.00	00.00	8.70	00.00	1.67	00.00	00.00	5.56	10.00	1.45	00.00
SEMI-MALNAD	**7.14**	**13.63**	**8.70**	**00.00**	**11.66**	**18.61**	**11.12**	**11.11**	**00.00**	**7.24**	**00.00**
Haliyal	7.14	13.63	8.70	00.00	5.00	13.96	11.12	5.56	00.00	5.80	00.00
Mundgod	00.00	00.00	00.00	00.00	6.66	4.65	00.00	5.55	00.00	1.44	00.00
District	100.00	100.00	100.00	100.00	100.00	100.00	100.00	100.00	100.00	100.00	100.00

Table 21 : North Kanara District-Small Industries

Sub-region and Taluka					Industries							
	Ceramics & glass	Chemicals	Ferrous & non Ferrous	Electricals	Food & beverage	General Engineering	Leather Rubber products	Paper Printing	Textile	Wood products	Misc.	Total
(1)	(2)	(3)	(4)	(5)	(6)	(7)	(8)	(9)	(10)	(11)	(12)	(13)
COASTAL	**11**	**13**	**14**	**2**	**36**	**13**	**5**	**14**	**8**	**45**	**6**	**167**
KARWAR	**2**	**8**	**10**	**2**	**8**	**5**	-	**2**	**2**	**12**	**2**	**53**
1.Karwar	2	6	5	1	4	3	-	2	-	3	2	28
2.Nandangadda	-	-	1	-	-	-	-	-	-	4	-	5
3.Kodibag	-	-	1	-	-	-	-	-	2	1	-	4
4.Sadashivgad	-	1	-	1	-	-	-	-	-	1	-	3
5.Baad	-	-	2	-	-	-	-	-	-	-	-	2
6.Kadwad	-	1	1	-	-	-	-	-	-	1	-	3
7.Kajubag	-	-	-	-	-	2	-	-	-	2	-	4
8.Binga	-	-	-	-	2	-	-	-	-	-	-	2
9.Kadiye	-	-	-	-	1	-	-	-	-	-	-	1
10.Sejwad	-	-	-	-	1	-	-	-	-	-	-	1
ANKOLA	**4**	**1**	**1**	-	**7**	**1**	**1**	**4**	**3**	**9**	-	**31**
1.Ankola	1	-	1	-	3	1	1	4	3	4	-	18
2.Belekeri	1	-	-	-	-	-	-	-	-	2	-	3
3.Soorve	-	1	-	-	1	-	-	-	-	-	-	2
4.Belamber	-	-	-	-	1	-	-	-	-	-	-	1
5.Baleguli	1	-	-	-	-	-	-	-	-	-	-	1
6.Agsur	1	-	-	-	-	-	-	-	-	-	-	1
7.Keni	-	-	-	-	2	-	-	-	-	-	-	2

(1)	(2)	(3)	(4)	(5)	(6)	(7)	(8)	(9)	(10)	(11)	(12)	(13)
8.Aversa	-	-	-	-	-	-	-	-	-	2	-	2
9.Manjguni	-	-	-	-	-	-	-	-	-	1	-	1
KUMTA	**3**	**1**	**2**	-	**6**	**2**	**1**	**5**	**1**	**15**	**1**	**37**
1. Kumta	2	1	1	-	3	2	-	5	1	12	1	28
2. Chitrigi	-	-	1	-	-	-	-	-	-	-	-	1
3. Hegde	-	-	-	-	2	-	-	-	-	-	-	2
4. Gokarn	-	-	-	-	-	-	-	-	-	1	-	1
5. Manki	-	-	-	-	-	-	-	-	-	2	-	2
6. Baad	1	-	-	-	-	-	-	-	-	-	-	1
7. Handigon	-	-	-	-	-	-	1	-	-	-	-	1
8. Divgi	-	-	-	-	1	-	-	-	-	-	-	1
HONAVAR	**1**	**1**	**1**	-	**8**	**2**	**3**	**3**	**2**	**8**	**3**	**32**
1. Honavar	-	1	1	-	4	2	3	3	2	5	2	23
2. Kasarkod	1	-	-	-	1	-	-	-	-	2	1	5
3. Haldipur	-	-	-	-	2	-	-	-	-	-	-	2
4. Baskeri	-	-	-	-	-	-	-	-	-	-	-	1
5. Kadtoka	-	-	-	-	1	-	-	-	-	-	-	1
BHATKAL	**1**	**2**	-	-	**7**	**3**	-	-	-	**1**	-	**14**
1. Bhatkal	1	1	-	-	2	1	-	-	-	1	-	6
2. Shirali	-	1	-	-	2	1	-	-	-	-	-	4
3. Rangikatta	-	-	-	-	1	1	-	-	-	-	-	2
4. Murdeshwar	-	-	-	-	1	-	-	-	-	-	-	1
5. Kaikini	-	-	-	-	1	-	-	-	-	-	-	1

MALNAD	**2**	**6**	**7**	**6**	**17**	**22**	**3**	**2**	**2**	**19**	**2**	**88**
SUPA	-	-	-	-	**1**	**1**	-	-	-	-	-	**2**
Supa	-	-	-	-	1	1	-	-	-	-	-	2
YELLAPUR	**1**	-	-	-	**1**	**2**	-	-	-	**2**	-	**6**
1. Yellapur	-	-	-	-	1	1	-	-	-	-	-	2
2. Devimarica	-	-	-	-	-	1	-	-	-	-	-	1
3. Kirwatti	-	-	-	-	-	-	-	-	-	1	-	1
4. Gullarpur	1	-	-	-	-	-	-	-	-	-	-	1
5. Mannigeri	-	-	-	-	-	-	-	-	-	1	-	1
SIRSI	**1**	**6**	**5**	**6**	**14**	**19**	**3**	**1**	**1**	**16**	**2**	**74**
1. Sirsi	1	5	5	6	14	18	3	1	1	14	2	70
2. Nilekani	-	1	-	-	-	-	-	-	-	1	-	2
3. Banavasi	-	-	-	-	-	1	-	-	-	-	-	1
4. Hutgar	-	-	-	-	-	-	-	-	-	1	-	1
SIDDAPUR	-	-	**2**	-	**1**	-	-	**1**	**1**	**1**	-	**6**
1. Siddapur	-	-	2	-	1	-	-	1	1	1	-	6
SEMI-MALNAD	**1**	**3**	**2**	-	**7**	**8**	**1**	**2**	-	**5**	-	**29**
HALIYAL	**1**	**3**	**2**	-	**3**	**6**	**1**	**1**	-	**4**	-	**21**
1. Dandeli	1	2	2	-	1	4	1	1	-	2	-	14
2. Haliyal	-	1	-	-	2	1	-	-	-	2	-	6
3. Tergaon	-	-	-	-	-	1	-	-	-	-	-	1

(1)	(2)	(3)	(4)	(5)	(6)	(7)	(8)	(9)	(10)	(11)	(12)	(13)
MUNDGOD	-	-	-	-	**4**	**2**	-	**1**	-	**1**	-	**8**
1. Mundgod	-	-	-	-	2	-	-	1	-	1	-	4
2. Pala	-	-	-	-	1	1	-	-	-	-	-	2
3. Malgi	-	-	-	-	1	1	-	-	-	-	-	2
District	14 (4.92)	22 (7.75)	23 (8.10)	8 (2.82)	60 (21.12)	43 (15.14)	9 (3.17)	18 (6.34)	10 (3.52)	69 (24.30)	8 (2.82)	284 (100.00)

Table 22 : North Kanara District - Types of Small Scale Industries

Ceramics and Glass : Roofing tiles, polished granite and other stones, sandalwood articles, earthen pots, glass articles, A.C. pipes.

Chemicals : Candles, washing soaps, amino plasts and phenol plasts, french polish, rice bran oil extraction, sea-shell powder, fish meal, burnt lime, distemper, bricks, scented sticks.

ferrous and Non-ferrous : Steel furniture, agricultural implements, plastic articles, paper bags, copper utensils, copper nails, buckets, gold and silver ornaments, window frames, steel trunks.

Electrical : All types of electrical items and repairs.

Food and beverages : Milk products, paddy milling, Ice-freezing of fish, rice and flour mill, vegetable oil and cakes such as of co-conut and groundnut, processed and scented betelnut, fruit juice and slices, cashewnut, cashewnut oil, biscuits and bread, soda water, jaggery.

General Engineering : Repairs of auto-mobiles, agricultural implements, servicing of pumpsets, welding.

Leather and Rubber Products : Rubber stamp, tyre retreading and tubes volcanising, leather chappals and shoes.

Paper and allied products : Exercise books, printing and binding, paper bags.

Textiles : Ready-made garments, blankets and sheets, saries, towels.

Wood products : timber cutting, sawing of timber and building materials, furniture, packing cases, hubs and spokes for carts, sandalwood carving, construction of boats, cane chairs and sofa sets, photo frames.

Miscellaneous : Stainless steel and hospital equipment, Managanese and iron ore production, coir fibre, coir ropes, umbrellas, combs and buttons, horns articles.

Relative importance of settlements as nodes to stimulate socio-economic development (Tables 23-24)

In 1977-78 there were 284 small scale industrial units in the District located in 54 settlements of which 37 (68.5 percent) are in the coastal tract, 11 (20.4 percent in the Malnad and 6 (11.1 percent) in the Semi-Malnad (Figs. 16-17). Most of the locations in the coastal tract - as could be expected, are in the coastal plain proper, while in the Malnad and the Semi-Malnad, these centres are very few and scattered. Also, the urban bias of these industrial units it quite distinct, in that nearly 73 percent of the total number of units is concentrated only in 12 out of 13 towns in contrast to 27 percent in the rural areas where 74.58 percent of the total population lives in

1283 villages. While Dandeli an industrial town in northern Malnad (47,625 population in 1981) has only 14 industrial units, Sirsi (38,907 population - 1981) located in the central part of the Malnad in the prosperous area of spices - paddy - forestry economy has 70 industrial units. The West Coast Paper Mills has contributed to the rapid growth of Dandeli and some clustering of small scale industrial units around it. Karwar, the District Headquarters (47,218 population) has only 28 industrial units. An overall observation from the distribution of industrial units indicates that no definite pattern of association other than preferential location in towns, availability of the raw materials and demand for the produce in urban centres seem to be the main criteria.

In the industrial structure of the District predominant industries are forest based (24.30 percent) and food processing (21.12 percent); and these two together claim about 45 percent of the total number of industries (Table 19). General engineering, Ferrous and non-ferrous industries, chemicals, paper and printing are also important. While the concentration of almost all industrial units except Electrical and General Engineering is most pronounced in the coastal tract, there is not much variation in the industrial structure among the three sub-regions in comparison with the District average. A few features of concentration of important industries are however noteworthy. Industrial units dealing with electricals are largely concentrated in the Malnad sub-region mainly in Sirsi town (75 percent of the total number of units). This is possibly due to the demand in the surrounding area because of the prosperity of the spice garden owners and also the town acting as trading centre. Likewise, ceramics and glass units are concentrated in the coastal region where silica, clay, firewood and other raw materials are available (78.6 percent of the total number of units). Units dealing with paper and printing also show preference to the coastal towns and villages where educational facilities are more in number and type. Industrial units dealing with chemicals and ferrous and non-ferrous items also show preferences to the coastal sub-region. Food processing, mainly dealing with rice and oil mills, processing of fish are concentrated in the coastal area on account of the regional concentration of these commodities. Textile units mainly dealing with ready-made garments and also weaving of cotton blankets, towels are a speciality of some centres in the coastal sub-region e.g. Nandangadda near Karwar. Contrary to the general expectation, wood based industries are dominant in the coastal area (particularly in port towns) and not so much in the heart of the forested area of the Malnad.

This aspect along with the flow of timber from the Malnad to other parts of Western India reveals the process of transformation of raw material rich areas into perpheries in the development process. As mentioned in the earlier pages, even during the historical past the Malnad in general has been an area of export of forestry and agricultural produce. Emergence of larger urban industrial centres such as Panaji-Marmagoa, Hubli, Shimoga and Mangalore further inhibits the process of industrialisation of the District.

All the 170 settlements comprising towns and villages of over 1000 population selected for this study have been evaluated in the context of their present and future possibilities for being designated as centres for providing social facilities and amenities and non-agricultural economic activities to promote integrated development of settlements and resources of the area. For this exercise composite score was worked out on the basis of demographic attributes, non-agricultural occupation, infrastructure facilities and amenities and industries. Appropriate weightages have been arrived at taking into account availability, type and levels of such attributes in all the settlements of over 1000 population. These weightages vary from 1.85 in the case of Primary school to 3083 for industries. (Table 23) There seems to be very little coordination among different departments in evolving a spatially integrated programme in the allocation of these attributes among different settlements.

Table 23 : Weightages for Social facilities and Economic Activities

Sl. No.	Services and Facilities	Weightage
1.EDUCATIONAL		
	(i) Primary School	1.85
	(ii) Middle School	3.96
	(iii) High School	16.92
2.MEDICAL		
	Health Centre, Dispensary, Hospitals	14.23
3.POSTAL		
	(P.O., P.T.O. and Phone)	4.69
4.COMMUNICATIONS (roads)		3.14
5.BANKS (Commercial)		23.69
6.INDUSTRY		30.83

Table 24 : North Kanara District - Population size and rank of settlements based on composite score

Settlements	By population Population	Rank	By composite score Rank	Value	No. of industrial units	Remark
(1)	(2)	(3)	(4)	(5)	(6)	(7)
Sirsi	28576	1	1	6739	70	Town
Karwar	27770	2	2	3326	28	Town (III)
Dandeli	25425	3	5	1674	14	Town (III)
Kumta	19112	4	3	2826	28	Town (III)
Bhatkal	18732	5	7	1205	6	Town (IV)
Honavar	12444	6	4	2149	23	Town (IV)
Haliyal	12163	7	9	925	6	Town (IV)
Gokarn (Km)	9547	8	16	234	1 (cultural)	Village-
Manki (Hn)	9224	9	17	232	2	"
Chitakula (Kr)	7801	10	24	149		"
Majali (Kr)	6286	11	32	112		"
Yellapur	6275	12	10	596	2	Town (IV)
Siddapur	6078	13	8	1085	6	Town (IV)
Hegde (Km)	5711	14	20	213	2	village
Bhavikeri (AK)	5558	15	48	69	-	"
Ankola	5505	16	6	1492	18	Town (IV)Tahsil Hq.
Mundgod	5,444	17	11	519	4	" (IV)
Kaikini (Bh)	5016	18	30	117	1	village
Shirali (Bh)	4645	19	15	325	4	
Shedgeri (Ak)	4596	20	35	99	-	"
Babruwada (Ak)	4029	21	71	45		Village

(1)	(2)	(3)	(4)	(5)	(6)	(7)
Banavasi (Si)	3881	22	72	45	1	Historical and-cultural village
Chendiye (Kr)	3831	23	51	64		
Mavalli II (Bh)	3798	24	67	49		
Avarsa (Ak)	3743	25	22	179	2	"
Tergaon (Hy)	3635	26	23	167	1	"
Belekeri (AK)	3597	27	13	392	3	"
Nandangadde (kr)	3586	28	14	335	5	
Heble (Bh)	3585	29	87	35		
Binga (kr)	3513	30	25	146	2	
Bailur (Bh)	3417	31	79	39		
Kadwad (Kr)	3397	32	16	319	3	
Kalambuli (Sp)	3315	33	37	93		
Mavalli-I (Bh)	3267	34	63	52		
Kinnar (Kr)	3232	35	43	80		
Kalbag (Km)	3194	36	81	38		
Amdalli (kr)	3193	37	46	72		
Baad (Kr)	3159	38	12	419	2	
Salkod (Hn)	3141	39	57	57		
Haldipur-I (Hn)	3039	40	31	114	2	
Kharwa (Hn)	3034	41	64	51		
Kagal (Km)	2058	42	68	49		
Shirali-II (Bh)	2951	43	45	79		
Kasarkod (Hn)	2893	44	17	277	5	
Belamber (Ak)	2812	45	39	85	1	
Mangalwad (Hy)	2769	46	91	31		
Hosakuli (Hn)	2714	47	53	58		
Kadtoka (Hn)	2580	48	44	80	1	
Bengre-I (Bh)	2529	49	101	27		
Mudgeri (Kr)	2513	50	88	35		

Arga (Kr)	2494	51	41	82	
Kadrigi (Hn)	2451	52	80	39	
Mavinkurve (Hn)	2435	53	85	36	
Murur (Km)	2406	54	69	49	
Holangadde (Km)	2400	55	92	30	
Mugwa (Hn)	2390	56	93	30	
Kampli (Yr)	2302	57	54	58	
Pala (Md)	2288	58	21	182	2
Balkur (Hn)	2269	59	134	20	
Haldipur-III(Hn)	2186	60	125	22	
Hiregutti (Km)	2157	61	34	100	
Kirwatti (Yr)	**2114**	**62**	**58**	**55**	
Belke (Bh)	2109	63	76	40	
Ghadsai (Kr)	2095	64	65	51	
Harwada (Ak)	2082	65	102	27	
Karki-II (Hn)	2079	66	103	27	
Nagarbastikeri(Hn)	2069	67	82	38	
Ambeli (Sp)	2054	68	50	65	
Nadumaskeri (Km)	2049	69	94	30	
Kusur (Md)	2029	70	36	99	
Aghanashini (Km)	2027	71	38	89	
Karki-I(Hn)	2015	72	61	53	
Nandikatta (Md)	1960	73	114	24	
Chigalli(Md)	1955	74	141	19	
Kathinkon(kr)	1946	75	118	23	
Hosur(Sd)	1942	76	55	58	
Navilgon(Hn)	1939	77	97	28	
Bengre-II (Bh)	1886	78	135	20	
Mirjan(Km)	1874	79	104	27	
Chandavar (Hn)	1861	80	40	84	
Hanehalli (km)	1807	81	74	42	
Hereangdi (Hn)	1790	82	98	28	

(1)	(2)	(3)	(4)	(5)	(6)	(7)
Belse (Ak)	1769	83	142	19		
Kelginoor (Hn)	1766	84	143	19		
Belwatgi (Hy)	1757	85	59	55		
Holegadde (Km)	752	86	52	59		
Badangod (Si)	1723	88	62	53		
Joida (Sp)	1703	87	62(a)	53		
Divgi (Km)	1660	89	42	81	1	
Hotegali (Kr)	1647	90	99	28		
Kekkar (Hn)	1646	91	144	19		
Hungunda (Md)	1642	92	162	13		
Hadinbal (Hn)	1640	93	82(a)	38		
Hospattan (Hn)	1638	94	149	18		
Jalavalli (Hn)	1626	95	105	27		
Yedoga (Hy)	1616	96	110	25		
Indur (Md)	1607	97	119	23		
Murkwad (Hy)	1592	98	33	101		
Shiralgi (Sd)	1576	99	106	27		
Gunvante (Hn)	1576	100	108	26		
Koppa (Bh)	1551	101	145	19		
Mainalli (Md)	1519	102	120	23		
Vandige (Ak)	1509	103	109	26		
Bachanki (Md)	1502	104	95	30		
Chikkankod (Hn)	1498	105	96	29		
Ulga (Kr)	1492	106	163	11		
Koppa (Md)	1476	107	89	33		
Haldipur-II (Hn)	1468	108	150	18		
Kawalwad (Hy)	1452	109	152	17		
Bargi (Km)	1449	110	121	23		
Kallabbe (Km)	1433	111	111	25		
Hillur (Ak)	1428	112	112	25		

Balikop (Sd)	1423	113	77	40	
Mudalli (Bh)	1394	114	122	23	
Sadashivalli(Si)	1379	115	107	27	
Shivalli (Si)	1373	116	60	55	
Kade (Hn)	1368	117	151	18	
Hankon (kr)	1365	118	100	28	
Kolsirsi (Sd)	1345	119	131	21	
Algeri (Ak)	1316	120	146	19	
Shirwad (Kr)	1311	121	113	25	1
Madnoor (Yr)	1309	122	132	21	
Bedkani (Sd)	1309	123	133	21	
Wailwada (kr)	1305	124	75	42	
Bhaire (Kr)	1296	125	115	24	
Kangod (Sd)	1292	126	49	68	
Kujalli (Km)	1268	127	126	22	
Jali (Bh)	1254	128	147	19	
Oralgi (Md)	1254	129	147 (a)	19	
Kodar (Kr)	1253	130	136	20	
Madhewada (Kr)	1251	131	127	22	
Tyrashi (Sd)	1248	132	137	20	
Hanchasta (Si)	1244	133	156	15	
Gotegali (Kr)	1240	134	28	133	
Agsur (Ak)	1240	135	123	23	1
Kelginidgunji (Hn)	1222	136	157	15	
Katur (Md)	1220	137	56	58	
Malgankoppa (Md)	1209	138	138	20	
Gudeangadi (Km)	1198	139	133 (a)	21	
Hosad (Hn)	1195	140	78	40	
Antralli (Km)	1190	141	128	22	
Malgi (Md)	1176	142	29	129	1
Shirur (Ak)	1176	143	155	16	
Tenkankeri (Ak)	1174	144	124	23	

(1)	(2)	(3)	(4)	(5)	(6)	(7)
Kodani (Hn)	1160	145	153	17		
Melinidgunji (Hn)	1153	146	26	144		
Jagalbet (Sp)	1148	147	73	44		
Nagre (Hn)	1145	148	113 (a)	25		
Gundolli (Hy)	1142	149	164	11		
Mallapur (Kr)	1132	150	139	20		
Kyadgi (Sd)	1129	151	27	134		
Tattihalli (Md)	1129	152	70	47		
Baad (Km)	1119	153	47	70	1	
Itagi (Sd)	1098	154	148	19		
Jawage (Hy)	1098	155	66	51		
Siddar (Kr)	1088	156	83	37		
Arlwad (Hy)	1085	157	160	14		
kalche (Yr)	1084	158	158	15		
Virnoli (Sp)	1069	159	116	24		
Madangeri (Km)	1062	160	86	36		
Bilgi (Sd)	1062	161	129	22		
Bhavikodla (Km)	1062	162	90	32		
kannadgal (Yr)	1059	163	130	22		
Achwale (Ak)	1058	164	113 (b)	25		
Hubbangeri (km)	1048	165	154	17		
Lukkeri (Km)	1034	166	165	9		
Pavinkurve (Hn)	1022	167	159	15		
Hichkad (Ak)	1015	168	72 (a)	45		
Todur (Kr)	1011	169	161	14		
Upponi (Hon)	1004	170	140	20		

* Settlements with industry are in bold letters.

Kr : Karwar Taluka   Sp : Supa Taluka   Ak : Ankola Taluka   Yr : Yellapur Taluka   Km : Kumta Taluka   Si : Sirsi Taluka
Hn : Honavar Taluka   Sd : Siddapur Taluka   Bh : Bhatkal Taluka   Md : Mundgod Taluka   Hy : Haliyal Taluka

The study bring out several interesting features related to the physical setting, situation with reference to the major transport routes linking towns within the District and space relations with the centres in the adjoining parts of Goa and South Kanara in the coastal region, Shimoga, Chikmagalur, Hassan and Coorg in the Malnad region of Karnataka of which the study area is a part and the major urban-industrial centres such as Hubli-Dharwar, Belgaum and Davangere in the Northern Maidan region. Only 54 out of 170 settlements have industrial component, however small, and most of them are of over 3500 population. The following are the important findings of the study.

i. Only two out of 8 towns - Sirsi (28,576 persons) and Karwar (27,770 persons) have maintained first and second rank both in respect of population and socio-economic activities. The anomaly is that Karwar, the District Headquarters has the second rank. This is because of its eccentric location with reference to the the rest of the area; in that Karwar is a port town situated at the extreme northern limit of the coastal plains. The town lost its importance as a port/trading centre with the coming of the railways linking Marmagoa and Hubli with Bombay. The town's proximity to rapidly growing area of Marmagoa-Panaji in Goa has been another disadvantage. Sirsi, on the other hand, has grown very rapidly surpassing Karwar though the former has been a contact town until 1950s situated at the edge of the Western Ghats along the through route connecting the coastal towns with Hubli in the Plateau. With improved accessibility and agricultural prosperity of the villages in the Malnad area, Sirsi, has acquired a prominent position as a centre of commerce and a few processing industries based on forest, wood and plantation crops - notably arecanut and pepper and horticulture (pineapple processing in particular).

ii. Administrative function has not necessarily provided all the tahsil headquarters the status of a town or a market/service centre. Thus, out of eleven tahsil headquarters only 8 of them are towns of which 3 are of class III level (20,000-50,000 persons), 4 are class IV towns (10,000-20,000 persons) and one town is of class V category (Yellapur, 6,275 persons).

The above analysis of infrastructure facilities and economic activities corroborates the hypothesis that the centrifugal forces at work on the economy of the District have weakened the basis of organisation of the economy which in its initial stages should by and large be centripetal to bring about spatial integration within. There are however some signs of reversal as is happening in part of the Malnad around Sirsi and in the coastal plains around Karwar though not according to a balanced pattern. Supa, Yellapur, are non-urban tahsil headquarters situated in the Malnad area while Mundgod is in the transitional or semi-Malnad area[2]. Inaccessibility and rugged terrain explain stagnation of Mundgod and Yellapur; while Supa has been in an area of Manganese mining and forested area in the northern part of the Malnad. Ankola in the coastal area too has an unfavourable location away from the sea on a ledge of laterite formations.

Dandeli, a Class III town has grown in the northern Malnad mainly as an industrial centre using forest wood for the manufacture of paper (West Coast Peper Mills) and other wood products. With rapidly dwindling forest resources the Paper Factory is depending for its raw materials on far flung areas upto Madhya Pradesh. The contrasts between the factory township and the market place are so striking that the town is not an integrated unit with a distinct rural hinterland as in the case of the commercial/market centres such as Sirsi.

iii. The coastal area though limited in its latitudinal extent has a number of centres of relatively larger population size (> 2000 population) and these are also functionally of higher rank in comparison with relatively few rural settlements of similar size in the foot-hill interiors or the Malnad. e.g. Gokarn (a religious centre), Majali, Avarsa, Binga and Banavasi (a historical/religious centre).

iv. Apart from the narrow coastal plains proper, there are small enclosed valley floors of alluvium built up by streams flowing down the spurs of the Western Ghats; and these are areas of large settlements which are of higher rank e.g. Mavalli and Shirali in Bhatkal Taluka and Manki and Idgunji (a famous temple settlement) in Honavar Taluka.

v. Transport routes connecting the towns both in the Coastal and Western Ghats area have provided, in places, transit centres which are relatively important and serve small sized settlements scattered in the hilly interiors. These settlements have population size of only about 1000 persons. This explains apparent anomalies in the population size and relative rank of settlements.

NOTES

1. The railway line was constructed not because of the importance of Dandeli (which is only a recently developed town) but on account of the importance of the northern Malnad area in the supply of valuable timber and wood products for railways and other uses in Western India.

2. Supa is now being evacuated as it would be sub-merged in one of the series of reservoirs being built under the Kali river Hydro-electricity Project.

SIX

Summary and Conclusions

This study of North Kanara District is by no means exhaustive and yet it is hoped that the main focus on spatial integration of development aspects analysed through the study of spatial structure and process of development has brought out some new findings on the basis of which *normative* spatial development strategy can be formulated and translated into a physical spatial framework of the District Plan.

In introducing the concept of Integrated Area Development the missing links in the present approach to planning at the Block and District Levels have been identified; in that the study area, and for that matter most parts of India, are essentially rural and the spatial dimension expresses itself in the configuration of the salient topographical features and the manner in which they have guided the spatial arrangement of human settlements, extent and types of landuses and cropping pattern and in turn influenced the spatial organisation of the economy. Within a small area of approximately 10,000 Km^2 the scarpline of the Western Ghats separates the coastal plains from the Hill region (the Malnad) proper; and within these two sub-regions the coastal foot hills and the Semi-Malnad tract are again distinct and show marked affinity to the larger sub-regions -(the coastal and the Malnad sub-regions of the State) in their functional-economic ties. Spatial integration of development has the following ecological and economic implications.

Resource development in the coastal plains needs integration as between large scale and intensive cultivation of paddy-pulses-groundnut in the sandy-alluvial plains proper and co-count gardens situated along the old sand dunes and the junction of lateritic hills and the sandy-alluvial plains. This requires the preparation of a land classification map on the scale of atleast 1:50,000 using the topographical map of the Survey of India of the same scale. There are also the problems of sand migration and saline marshes nearer the river mouths. Such areas should be the basis for drainage and soil conservation measures by proper bunding. These should form the on-going programmes under the National Rural Employment Programme (NREP) and of the Integrated Rural Development programme for creating durable assets[1].

In the Malnad and the Semi-Malnad area, forest and agriculture-particularly of plantation crops are inter-woven in that forest lands close to garden area supply green leaf manure for the latter. Besides, forest and water resources need to be conserved and their use ought to complementary and not competitive both for local use and for consumption outside the District. There is a need to prepare a spatial development strategy for the *Malnad* region of Karnataka as a whole in relation to the long term strategy for the development of different sub-regions of Karnataka (Coastal, Malnad, Northern Maidan and the Southern Maidan). From such a strategy the priorities for development of resources of North Kanara District in relation to its local and regional priorities can be better evaluated (Fig. 18). Exploitation of river waters of the Malnad region on an *ad hoc* basis with emphasis on state level priorities without evaluating its impact on the environment and the economy of the people who inhabit the region has resulted in strong regional identity expressed through their mode of cultivation and socio-cultural ties within the region. This is a healthy trend and needs to be strengthened rather than providing political overtones which might give way to regionalism based on caste and communal conflicts as are happening elsewhere. A popular movement is underway to "save North Kanara District from the devastating consequences" of the six major hydro projects of which the Kali Nadi Project has been in the process of implementation[2]. These hydro-power projects produce nearly 2,201 MW of power for consumption largely outside the District[3]. Paradoxically, while the coastal and the Malnad sub-regions face acute scarcity of drinking water and for intensive agriculture, much of the water after its use for generating electricity through gravitational fall on the Western side of the Ghats is wasted as it flows into the Arabian Sea. Integrated land and water use plan (for irrigation, industrial and domestic use) needs to be drawn up as a physical spatial plan.

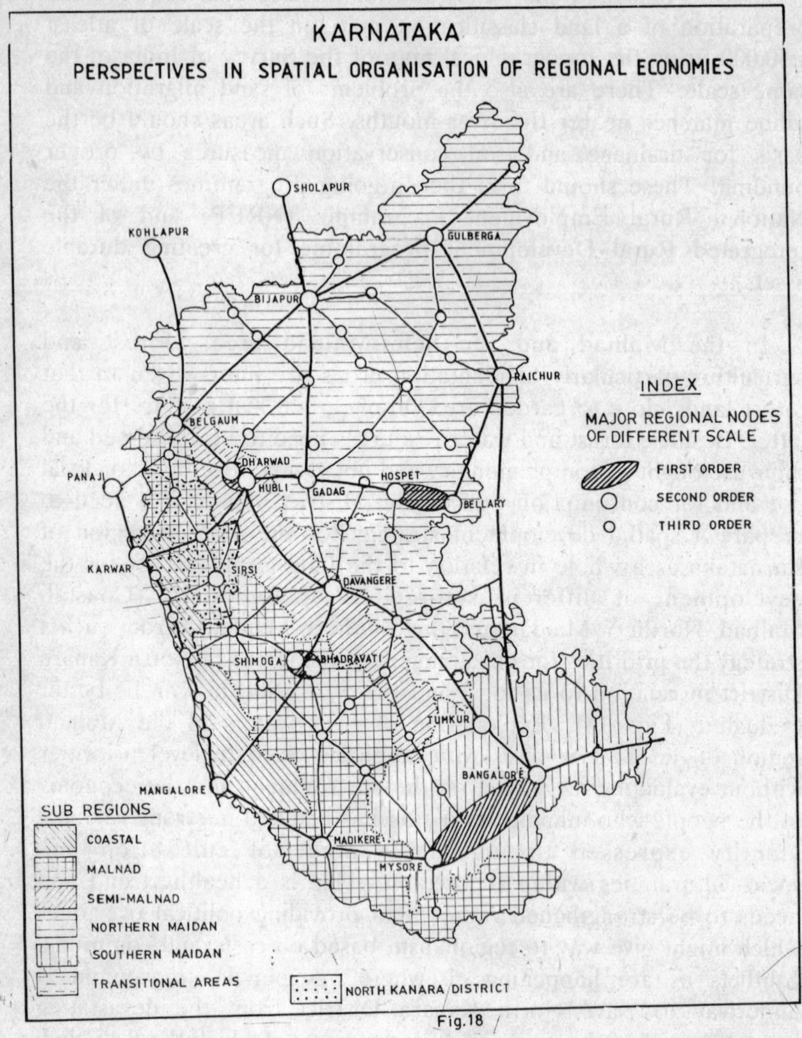

Fig.18

The resource base is diversified with distinct spatial affinity and lends itself for the development of industries rooted to fishery, forest, spices and plantations and minerals - (notably manganese and some low grade iron ore). In the coastal foot hill areas laterites as building materials await systematic quarrying and in places lateritic clay has been made use of for the manufacture of tiles and toys. Artisans using sandalwood, coir and bamboo for export of their produce, though few, show potentiality for the development of these small scale industries in an organised manner.

While demographic attributes of population are marked by low density, out migration (particularly of male population) and spatial contrast in their distribution, the literacy is high (for both male and female) inspite of the disadvantages of small sized and scattered settlements in the foot hill area of the coastal sub-region and the Malnad. This has a legacy of the past in that the District was a part of the better administered territory - the Bombay Province. Creation of employment opportunities for the educated youth needs priority in the context of industrial development in the District. Fishery and other light industries (mostly in the existing port-towns and other urban centres) need to be developed by proper assessment of the local resources.

Establishment of growth centres - as envisaged in the Five Year Plans has to be evaluated in the context of nodality as the basis of spatial organisation of the economy. Growth centre strategy adopted in the context of initiating the trickling down process of benefits of economic planning has not produced desired result because the factors that contribute to growth and the channels through which they diffuse (usually a system of nodes and the communication lines that radiate from them) are not assessed a part of the development process taking place in the geographic space.

Spatial organisation around nodes is the weaker link in the economy of the District. This is partly because the District has never been under one administrative rule; and even in the coastal tract the small port towns had very limited hinterland; and these were physically separated by unbridged rivers.Similarly, in the Malnad and the Semi-Malnad important trading centres like Sirsi or the industrial town like Dandeli did not have economic links with the surrounding areas. As the findings of the study reveal, the gaps in functional-economic status as between towns of the District and those in the adjoining District are very wide and in the emerging pattern of linkages north-south axis is getting stronger as a result of the construction of the national highway. Port-towns such as Karwar, (District Headquarters) Kumta, Honavar and Bhatkal need economic inputs to match the available infrastructure and the quality of human resources. The naval base proposed at Karwar could be only a beginning for raising the status of the port-town to that of an urban industrial centre.

Analysis of the settlements and their attributes-social and economic - revealed the gaps as between towns and rural settlements on the one hand and among rural settlements in the population range of 1,000 - 3,500 persons. It would appear that a twin strategy using nodality as well as pockets of valley floors in the coastal and the Malnad area of small settlements as 'nodal regions' need to be adopted for spatial integration of development programmes.

The District Headquarters - Karwar has a peripheral location; so also is the case of Dandeli the industrial town in the Malnad. While in terms of average area and population the District fulfills the conditions for being treated as a planning unit its spatial pattern and structure of small villages necessitate consideration of the coastal and the Malnad sub-regions (comprising groups of taluka) as distinct units for spatial integration of development plans. Such a strategy would be more realistic than the use of Development Blocks (equivalent to taluka) and the District as planning units. The coastal sub-region comprises river basins of the Kali, Gangavali, Aghanashini and the Sharvati and it would also be possible to use them for preparing normative spatial models of integration development of resources river-basin wise. In the Malnad on the other hand, a series of micro-water sheds would provide recurring patterns of development norms with a micro-hydel/water project at the head waters region ensuring waster and power to the narrow valley floors so rich in forest and plantation agriculture with small and scattered settlements clinging to them and the transport routes passing through these valleys to the trading towns in the region.

NOTES

1. This is one such example by way of illustration. Others are afforestation of lateritic uplands, horticulture and raising of fodder crops in the foothill interiors.

2. The movement is on two fronts; one is on the model of *Chipko movement* (*Appiko movement* in local language, to save trees from indiscriminate felling by contractors and others) and the second one is to save valuable forest wealth, agricultural land and displacement of local inhabitants from large scale sub-mergence by the construction of reservoirs for producing hydro-electricity.

3. While hydro-electricity is cheap for production, the total cost involved including loss of valuable forest and garden lands is heavy. Benefit cost analysis brings out the ratio as 0.57 (Paranjpe, V. : *Bedthi - I Hydro Electricity Project in North Kanara : An Economic Analysis"* Seminar on Hydro-Projects in North Kanara Sirsi, 1981 Mimeo.

REFERENCES

Abler R.et. al (1967) *Spatial Organisation*, Prentice Hall, New Jersey.

Alam M. et. al(1982) *Settlement system of India*, Oxford and IBH Publishing Co. New Delhi.

Berry. B.J.L. and Garrison. W. (1958) "The Functional Basis of Central Place Hierarchy" *Economic Geography* Vol. 34 pp. 145-154.

Berry, B.J.L. (1967) *Spatial Analysis - A Reader in Statistical Geography*, Prentice Hall, Englewood Cliffs, New Jersey.

Berry, B.J.L. (1967) *Geography of Market Centres and Retail Distribution* Englewood Cliffs: Prentice Hall.

Bhagat, D.G. (1960) "Regional concept for highway planning - the web lattice pattern" *Journal of the Indian Roads Congress*, Vol. XXIV Part 4 and Volume XXIV Part 5, pp. 629-665.

Bhat, L.S. (1972) *Regional Planning in India* Statistical Publishing Society, Indian Statistical Institute, Calcutta.

Bhat, L.S. (1976) *Micro-Level Planning - A Case study of Karnal Area, Haryana, India,* Rajesh Publications, New Delhi.

Blaikie, P.M. (1971) "Spatial organisation of Agriculture in Some North Indian Villages" *Trans. Inst. British Geographers* 50 : p. 1-40.

Bombay Gazetteers *North Kanara District Gazetteer.*

Chisholm M. (1966) *Geography and Economics*, Bell, London

Chorley, R.J. and Haggett, P. (1967) *Model in Geography*, Methuen, London

Christaller, W. (1933) *The Central Places in Southern Germany* translated by C.W. Baskin, Englewood Cliffs : Prentice Hall

Deshpande. C.D. (1948) *Western India - A Regional Geography*, students' Own Book Depot. Dharwar.

Deshpande, C.D. and Bhat, L.S. et. al. (1980) *Impact of a Metropolitan City on the Surrounding Region* : A study of South Kolaba, Maharashtra, Concept Publishing Company, New Delhi.

Friedmann, J.R.P. (1966) *Regional Development Policy - A Case Study of Venezuela*, M.I.T. Press Cambridge, Mass.

Gadgil, D.R. (1967) *District Development Planning, Gokhale* Institute of Politics and Economics.

Geddes Patrick (1949) *Cities in Evolution*, London

Glikson A. (1955) *Regional Planning and Development*, Netherlands Universities Foundation for International Co-operation, Molenstraat, The Hague.

Government of India Planning Commission (1973) *District Planning*, New Delhi

Government of India, Planning Commission (1984) *Report of the Working Group on District Planning*, Vols. I and II, New Delhi.

Government of India, Planning Commission (1973) *Report of the Task Force on Integrated Rural Development*, New Delhi.

Government of India, Planning Commission (1985) *The Seventh Five Year Plan* 1985-90, Vol. I and II, New Delhi.

Haggett, P. (1965) *Locational Analysis in Human Geography*, Edward Arnold, London

Hoyle, B.S. ed. (1974) *Spatial aspect of Development*, John Wiley, London.

Indian Council of Social Science Research (1972) *Survey of Research in Geography*, New Delhi, Popular Prakashan, Bombay.

Johnson, E.A.J. (1970) *The organisation of space in developing countries*, Harvard University Press.

Kundu, A. and Raza Moonis (1982) *India Economy - the Regional Dimension* Centre for the Study of Regional Development, Jawaharlal Nehru University, New Delhi.

Learmonth, A.T.A. (1962) *Sample Villages in Mysore State, India* Department of Geography, The University of Liverpool, Liverpool.

Learmonth, A.T.A. and Bhat, L.S. (eds.) (1960) *Mysore State - Vol. I : Atlas of Resources* Asia Publishing House, Bombay

Learmonth, A.T.A. et. al. (1962) Mysore State - Vol. II : A Regional Synthesis, Asia Publishing House, Bombay.

Losch, A. (1954) *The Economics of Location*, Translation by W.H. Woglom, Yale University Press, Boston.

Misra, R.P. et.al. ed. (1969) *Regionl Planning Concepts, Techniques,*

Policies and case Studies, Prasaranga, Mysore University.

Misra, R.P. et. al. ed. (1980) *Regional Development, Essays in Honour of M. Honjo Maruzan*, Hongkong.

Philbrick, A.K. (1957) "Principles of Areal Functional Organisation in Regional Human Geography" *Economic Geography*, Vol. 33, pp. 299-336.

Ramachandran, H. (1980) *Village clusters and Rural Development*, Concept Publishing Company, New Delhi.

Rao, V.L.S.P. (1964) *Regional Planning*, Asia Publishing House, Bombay.

Rao, V.L.S.P. and Bhat, L.S. (1960) *Planning Regions in the Mysore State* the need for re-adjustment of District boundaries, Indian Statistical Institute, Calcutta.

Rao, V.L.S.P. (1983) *Urbanisation in India* - Spatial Dimensions, Concept Publishing Company, New Delhi.

Silva, S. (1957) *Malnad or Male Nadu*. All India Malnad Third Conference, Sirsi, North Kanara.

Sopher David (ed.) (1980) *An exploration of India* - Geographical Perspectives on Society and Culture, Longman, London.

Spate O.H.K. and Learmonth, A.T.A. (1967) *India and Pakistan*, Methuen, London

Sunderam, K.V. ed. (1985) *Geography and Planning* Essays in honour of V.L.S. Prakasa Rao, Concept Publishing Company, New Delhi.

Whyte R.O. (1982) *The Spatial Geography of Rural Economies*, Oxford University Press, Bombay.

SOURCES TO DATA AND MAPS

1. Census of India (1971) *Mysore - General Population Tables*, Series - 14, Part II-A.
2. Census of India (1971) *Mysore General Report Part I-A, Vol. II* Series -14.
3. Census of India (1971) *District Census Hand Book - North Kanara District* Series 14.
4. Census of India (1981) *Karnataka - General Population Tables* Part II-A.
5. Census of India (1981) *Karnataka - Primary Census Abstract* - General Population Part II-B (i).
6. Government of Karnataka (1976) *Talukawise Plan Statistics*, District and Regional Planning Unit, Planning Department.
7. Government of Karnataka Bureau of Economics and Statistics,

Uttara Kannada District (1977-78) *An Economic Review*, District Statistical Office, Karwar.

8. Government of Karnataka, Mysore Power Corporation Ltd. (1978) *Kalinadi Hydro-Electric Project*, Dandeli
9. Survey of India *Topographical Maps of 1"* : 1 Mile and 1" 4 Miles covering North Kanara District and adjoining area.

INDEX

Administrative function, 89
Aghanashini river, 31, 96
Agricultural Land Use, 34; occupation, 82; produce, 21, 23, 24
Agriculture and processing activities, 15
Agronomic conditions, 13
Amenities, 52, 61; and industries, 64
Ankola, 50, 57
Arab, 25
Archaean gneisses, 29
Banavasi, 53, 64
Bangalore, 21, 22, 48
Banking facilities, 71-72
Barren sand dunes, afforestation of, 37-38
Bedit River Power Project, 37
Bhat, L. S, 32
Bhatkal taluka, 25,40, 43, 46, 57
Bihar, 13
Bilgi, 27, 64
Bombay, 21, 24
Central Place theory, 16
Chikamagalur, 89
Chitakul, 25
Climatic conditions, 45-46
Coastal plains, agricultural labourers of, 50; characteristics of, 48
Commercial crops, 27
Computer facilities, 17
Coorg, 89
Cropping pattern, 23, 37, 62
Dandeli (Haliyal taluka), 44, 61; West Coast Paper Mills at, 73
Deep gullies, formation of, 31-33
Demographic attributes, 82
Development programmes, spatial integration of, 14, 96-97
Double cropped areas, 22
Ecological and economic implications, 92
Economic activities, spatial organisation of, 17, 64
Education, facilities for, 21, 68, 81
Electric facilities, 67
Employment opportunities, creation of, 95
Environment, aspects of, 48
Erosion, problem of, 23
Exploitation, 43, 61, 93; initial level of, 63
Export of fish, 43
Exports, 25
First Five Year Plan, 13, 24, 95
Food poisoning, 25; processing, 81-82
Foot loose, 17
Forest and plantation products, 57; water resources, 93; produce, 41; resources, development of, 41-42
Forestry and agricultural produce, export of, 82
Formal economy, functional organisation of, 14
Functional economic linkages, new pattern of, 64-65; entity, 18
Gangavali-Bedit, 31
Garden crops, 37
Goa, 20
Gokarna, 27
Haggett, P., 14
Haidar Ali, 24
Haliya taluka, 44, 48, 61
Haryana, 13
Hassan, 89
Health facilities, 71
Higher educational facilitiy, 68-70
Honavar, 25, 43, 57
Housing colonies, 48
Hubli, 25

Human resources, 62. 63; quality of, 95-96
Hydro-electric project, construction of, 45-46
Hydro-power development, 61 resources, 67; projects, 93
Industrial structure, 73, 81
Inland trading centres, 26
Infrastructural amenities, 16; facilities, 52, 61, 64, 65; analysis of, 89
Integrated Area Development, 92; strategy of, 18-24; Planning, 13-17; Analytical framework for, 16-20
Integrated Rural Development, programme, 17-18
Inter-regional interactions, 63; variations, 40
Isard, W., 14
Joga falls, 31
Kali Hydro-electric Project, 24
Kali Nadi Project, 24, 31, 37, 93
Kanya Kumari, 27
Karnataka, 20, 89
Karwar, (port town), 25, 57, 61, 68, 90
Kerala, 13, 29
Konkan coast, 20, 29
Kudremukh, 31
Kumta (small port), 25, 43, 68
Land classification, 93
Landforms, 32
Landuse and cropping pattern, 62, 92
Learmonth, A. T. A., 32
Linear belt, 53; pattern, 53
Literacy, level of, 50; pattern of, 50-52
Loasch, A., 14
Madhya Pradesh, 44, 90
Madras Province, 24
Maharashtra, 13, 20, 29
Malaria, eradication of, 21
Malnad tracts, 25, 27, 31, 41, 53, 89
Mangalore, 27
Marriage migration, 21-22
Marshy land, formation of, 37
Mineral resources, 42-43
Mundagod, 51, 90
National Rural Employment Programme (NREP), 17, 93
Nodal regions, 96
North Kanara District, 92; Sex ratio, 49; Distribution of population, 55; Health facilities, 71; population size, 83; regional characteristics, 74; Small Scale Industries, 76
Objectives, formulation of, 14
On-going programmes, 93
Outmigration, 49
Panaji, 27
Patrick Geddes, valley section of, 14
Peninsular plateau, 29
Physical landscape, 32; chracteristics of,34-36 setting, 29
Plantation crops, 26, 32, 66, 89, 93; economy, 21-25
Population density, 20-22
Port-towns, 95
Ports handled commodities, 25
Portuguese Territory, 24, 25
Postal facilities, 71-72
Promote integrated development, 82
Pumpset for irrigation, 67
Raw material, transformation of, 81, 82-84
Regional development planning, 13; problem of, 16
Reorganisation states, 27-30
Resource base, 34; development, 92-93
Rural Settlements,52; distribution of,52-53
Rural-urban integration, 15
Salt production, 43
Sandy-alluvial plains, 92
Sectoral targets, 16
Semi Malnad, 32, 34; transitional character, 53; tract, 32
Sharawati river, 24, 31, 37, 96
Shimoga, 64
Siddapur taluka, 25, 27, 32, 40, 64
Sirsi, 25, 27, 32, 40, 98, 61, 64, 68
Small Farmer Development Agency, 17
Small scale industrial units, 76, 81; pattern of concentration of, 75-78
Social facilities, 17
Socio-economic interaction, 25-30
South Kanara District, 27
Space economy, 14
Spatial development strategy, 93; integration, basis for, 15; Variations, population density, 48
Supa Taluka, 41, 46, 48, 90
Third Five Year Plans, 13
Traditional agricultural economy, 57
Transport routes, 90-91
Urban settlements, 56-57
Urbanisation, level of, 20; pattern of, 56, 57
Vijyanagar, 27
Water and power resources, exploitation of, 67-68
Water resources, utilisation of, 43
West coast highway, 66, 67; regions, configuration, 29-30
West coast paper mills, 73, 90
Western Ghats (Malnad), 22, 24; spatial development framework, 24-26
Yellapur, 25, 27, 32, 40, 41, 43, 46, 57, 90